ᴸᴱᴱᴰ'S CO

9

Pasts and Futures
or
What is history for?

Pasts and futures
or
What is history for?

Jean Chesneaux

Thames and Hudson

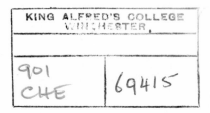
Translated from the French *Du passé faisons table rase?* by
Schofield Coryell

Text set in 10/12 pt IBM Press Roman, printed by photo-
lithography, and bound in Great Britain at The Pitman Press,
Bath.

Contents

Foreword

Geoffrey Barraclough

This is a book about Historical Truth — and (how could it not be?) about its big bouncing ugly sister, Historical Myth. Not, I hasten to add, another of those logic-chopping disquisitions about the philosophy of history, or the desultory reflections of an armchair historian ruminating about his craft. Jean Chesneaux is, indeed, a well-known professional historian, an expert on modern China and Vietnam; he has made his way to the top of the academic ladder. But that, he tells us, is something he has put behind him, a closed chapter in his life, and his new book tells us why.

If this were simply another discussion of 'the crisis of conventional history', it would be reasonable to ask what more there is to say on that tired and threadbare subject. What Chesneaux offers us is something entirely different. His new book is an intensely personal document, almost a chapter of autobiography, 'a work of self-criticism' and an 'expression of my uncertainties'. It is also, in a very real sense, a political document; indeed, one of Chesneaux's central tenets is the impossibility of drawing a line between history and politics, his rejection of the claim of historians to stand dispassionately above the fray and adjudicate events impartially and objectively from outside. Chesneaux belongs to the political family for which 1968 was a year of destiny. What his book tells us is how the experience and anguish of 1968 changed his attitude to history and to politics, to the Communist Party (of which he was a member for twenty-one years) and to the 'history Establishment'.

Unlike some other veterans of '68, who have made their peace with the system and are now settled quietly in safe routine jobs, administering and broadcasting, Chesneaux is an angry, dissatisfied man. Angry, in the first place, with himself for accepting so long 'the double conditioning of "Party" and "career"'; angry still more with the 'history Establishment', those 'willing accomplices of advanced technocratic capitalism'; — but angry most of all at the yawning gap (as he sees it) between history as it is and history as it can and should be. For Chesneaux (not to mince words) history as it is — the history, that is to say, taught in schools and universities and served up in our history books — is a whore, up for sale to the highest bidder, and historians are little better than a gang of whoremongers. This, it will be evident, is an angry book, more likely to make enemies than to make friends. The danger is that it will be written off as the work of a fanatic or crank.

Chesneaux is angry at the distortions and suppressions which make up our conventional picture of the past. He cites the example of the 'Occitans' of southern France, deprived of their history because their struggles for autonomy do not fit the myth of a 'majestic' centralized French 'nation-state' constructed by Richelieu, Louis XIV and Napoleon. Or the Cherokees in the United States whose few remaining historical sites are to be flooded to build a dam. Or the Australian aborigines, compelled in 1970 to listen to 'Bicentennial' celebrations, as though Australia had no history before the arrival of Captain Cook. From this angle, what is history but the propaganda of the victors? But this manipulation of history is not the worst. Even the 'primary sources' on which historians set such store are tainted and suspect. Our historical memory is shaped by the 'power structure' and its 'gigantic recording machine'. From ancient Babylon onwards, *their* tax-lists, *their* censuses, *their* parish registers, *their* legal records, provide us with the information *they* want. Or withhold it, if need be, as the Chinese mandarin historians covered up the history of Chinese peasant revolts.

And then the historians, the professional scribes and pharisees! How revealing their language, or what Chesneaux prefers to call their 'rhetoric'! Revolutionaries appear as 'agitators', revolts as 'disorders' — the very language of government, for which any form of protest, any dissatisfaction with things as they are, has to be played down and minimized. But even more pernicious is their obsession with continuity, their awesome respect for the 'subtle alchemy' which binds society together; for what is continuity but the continuity of the apparatus of repression? As though history were not made up of discontinuities, of revolutions, catastrophes and civilizations which perished in the sand! In any event, their obsession with continuity puts them on the side of the powers that be, conscious or unconscious upholders of the *status quo*, at best timid supporters of step-by-step evolutionary change within the existing system, but never advocates of a revolutionary break. To snap the magic thread which holds world history together — even if the thread is compounded of extortion, oppression and exploitation — that, for them, is the ultimate sin.

Against this farago of myth, half-truth and deliberate distortion, Chesneaux sets up a vision of history inspired directly by the theoretical legacy of Marxism. Many writers in the past have criticized the pretensions of conventional history. Nietzsche tore to pieces the historian's claim to objectivity. Herzen declaimed against historians whose purpose is 'to arrest the future by means of the past'. And was it not Matthew Arnold who described history as a 'huge Mississippi of falsehood'? What distinguishes Chesneaux's critique from theirs is his consistent, undeviating commitment to Marxism. Not, of course, the 'vulgar, dogmatic Marxism' of Marxist academics, who degrade Marxism 'to the level of economic fatalism'. For them he has nothing but scorn. Marxism, Chesneaux correctly observes, is not a 'theory of history' but a call to action, and in that action history has a vital part to play. It is 'never neutral — never above the battle'. To define the future, he says, you need a past. The past is not an inanimate object; it is 'a political issue, a theme of struggle'.

To combat the 'reactionary cult of the past', Chesneaux argues, we need a revolutionary cult of the past. If there is no such thing as ideological neutrality, if the much vaunted objectivity of history is a myth — and I, for one, find it hard to quarrel with him on this score — why should one side have it all its own way? Against a history of the right you must have a history of the left; against a history written from the point of view of the possessing classes you must set a history written from the point of view of the working classes. Plausible, perhaps, but disquieting also. Is history merely a shuttlecock, tossed about incessantly between the contending parties? Chesneaux's answer is that only the exploiters have anything to gain by distorting history; the working class has 'nothing to hide'. I wonder: if Clio is a whore, she may also be a proletarian whore. They exist.

Chesneaux is on firmer ground when he assails the professional historian's incessant preoccupation with the past 'for its own sake'. Most people ask what history is *about*; Chesneaux asks what it is *for*. The bourgeois historian's answer to this question is characteristic: it widens our perspectives, 'enlarges the area of individual experience', provides new insights and 'a new level of wisdom'. All perhaps true; but is it not also a typical expression of quietism and resignation, reminiscent of the monks who pondered eternity in the fastnesses of their monasteries while Rome burnt? Chesneaux is right. The past is as dead as the men who made it. The only reason — beyond sheer antiquarianism — to be concerned with the past is to gain insight into the present and a glimpse of possible futures. But they are only possible futures, and the real future will be what we choose to make it. History, as Marx warned us, provides no answers and will not fight our battles for us. By itself history does nothing; it is men — 'real, living men', fighting for their ideals — on whom the outcome will depend.

Chesneaux's ultimate purpose, I suspect, was to drive that lesson home. He has written (as he admits) an untidy, unfinished book, but for the professional historian it is also a disquieting book, posing questions it is easier to evade than answer. For myself, at least, it has shattered any lingering belief in the neutrality of history, and forced me to rethink what we are about. And what of the general reader (if that phantom of the bookseller's imagination really exists)? For him or her, I think, the important thing is not to reflect on history, but to reflect on the world in which we live. Without history, perhaps, we shall never come to terms with that world, because the past (as Chesneaux says) is a 'reference-point' that makes possible 'a radical critique of the present' and 'the definition of a qualitatively different future'. But history is only a gateway, a port of entrance, and what is important is what we do when we get to the other side.

Introduction

The author of this essay on historical knowledge is a professional historian (un)comfortably settled in his academic chair. Yet he hopes to go beyond the kind of general remarks about history that his 'colleagues' have been in the habit of publishing these past few years, never trying to transcend the circumscribed limits of the historian's conventional 'territory' and universe of discourse. What is the role of historical knowledge in society? Does it play in favour of, or against, the existing social order? Is it an élitist product that descends from the specialists to the 'consumers' of history by way of books, television and tourism? Or is it rooted, from the outset, in a *collective need*, an active relationship to the past affecting the entire society, specialized research being but one of its many aspects? Such questions are clearly political.

For that reason, I have attempted to approach them in directly political terms, from the dual standpoint of an overall anticapitalist outlook and the experience of personal participation in the concrete struggles of recent years. In other words, from a position that is both Marxist and communist, however loose and ambiguous those two terms may be. And despite the handicap that my privileged academic situation and its accompanying social isolation represents for anyone engaged in political deliberation of this type, I have tried both to reason historically about the society with which we are all confronted and to reflect on the basic problems of historical knowledge – the scientific nature of such knowledge, the objectivity and limitations of documents and techniques, the relationship between current events and the long-range view, the place of history in geopolitical space and in the world of nature, the obstacles to the attainment of a genuinely universal history. This is why references to political realities and active struggles are no less frequent in this book than scholarly references to the writings of other historians. Such struggles are the soil from which historical thinking can grow. *They are its basic reason for being*; they alone make it necessary and legitimate.

Nearly all my 'colleagues' are willing and even eager to live in a state of dual personality. As historians, they are neutral, objective, scientific – within the profession, the anti-imperialistic militant rubs elbows with the ex-communist who has succeeded in marketing his apostasy and is a favourite of the C.I.A. But everyone has a right, as a 'private' individual, to his own political 'options' that his colleagues respect as a matter of principle – and that are supposedly irrelevant to his 'scientific work'. In these pages, this conventional separation is rejected and deliberately overturned.

This attempt to clarify politically the problems of historical knowledge is inspired by the theoretical legacy of Marxism, viewed not as a dogma but as a process of 'constant creation' in Gramsci's sense; by the contributions of the Chinese Revolution, whatever its contradictions (the 'struggle between two lines') and its theoretical reticence; and by the concrete experience of Western leftism, post-May '68 in France or the American 'New Left'. The time has come to attempt a synthesis of these varied experiences and achievements, and I hope my own critique of the academic historians and their work will be a modest contribution to that attempt. A partial and tentative contribution, of course, but one that is certainly not in the doctrinaire spirit of those armchair Marxists who ceaselessly feed on theoretical slogans and scholarly references at a safe distance from the people's struggles and their concrete demands. Nor in the spirit of those veterans of intellectual leftism whose sneering cynicism and destructive contempt are unacceptable – the 'disillusioned ones' who take refuge in the metaphysics of rebellion and try to flee all dogmatism by throwing out Marx along with the dirty bathwater; in their rejection of so-called proletarian idealism, they 'thrust themselves into intellectual gimmicks or take shelter in mystical illuminations,' as our friends of the left-wing review, *Révoltes Logiques*, so aptly put it.

'For whom are you writing?' asked Lu Xun. That is 'the basic question, a question of principle', says a poster on sale in every Peking bookstore. Yet not many historians begin their works with an attempt to define their purpose. They simply assume that they are writing first for their 'peers', then for the intelligent 'general reader' who is willing and able to be educated by professional historians.

I am speaking here to other historians – mainly those who are uncomfortable in their profession and in the academic world in general because they are uncomfortable in the capitalist society, which does not necessarily mean that they feel at home in the structures of the 'organized' Left or Far Left. These intellectuals who find themselves in a state of more or less latent conflict with the Establishment have a role to play in the common struggle. Historians, like other intellectuals, cannot passively wait until capitalist culture and society have disappeared to raise questions about their own speciality and its place in the political struggle. Let us hope they will not do this while remaining comfortably within their own closed circle.

History is an intellectual discipline that touches an extremely broad audience: the millions of pupils studying their text-books; television viewers choosing their programmes; readers of mass-circulation magazines; tourists visiting castles or cathedrals. It is to them, of course, that I should address my remarks and with them that I should be discussing the traps of the historian's rhetoric. But this is merely wishful thinking, in view of the way intellectuals in our society — excepting those who are in favour with the Establishment media — are cut off from the rest of the people. The invisible doors of our universities are as hermetically sealed as those of the factories, housing projects, nuclear plants, or hospital complexes.

The past is both a stake in current struggles and an essential factor in the political relationship of forces. Yet in the 'movement' — meaning all who act against the existing system, whether as 'organized' militants or independents — little attention is given to the traps of the prevailing historical rhetoric. 'Let us make a clean slate of the past' may be our motto, but we accept too easily the false assumptions of conventional history, the chronological slicing-up of past experience, the taste for narratives in the past tense, the authority of the printed word, the isolation of documents and problems from their context, the uncritical use of the specialist's work. My hope is to encourage those engaged in ongoing social and political struggles — workers, ecologists, women, etc. — to reject the Establishment version of historical knowledge. Let them build their own relationship to the past on the basis of what they have gone through together, their common experience and needs, taking their own past as the starting-point for this fundamental rethinking. Let us reverse the hierarchical relationship between past and present, between historical specialists and non-specialists, in our quest for the type of history the revolutionary struggle requires.

Historians are not the only ones in today's world to confront problems arising from their professional intellectual activity in the social context of their work and their life situation. They are not the only ones to feel disturbed and to seek a radical revision of élitist science. French left-wing physicists have launched a magazine, *Impascience*, to express their view that a certain type of 'science' is a dead end ('impasse') from which they are impatiently striving to extricate themselves. Geographers train the spotlight of their criticism on the 'geography of the mandarins and experts', those willing accomplices of advanced technocratic capitalism, efficient cogs in the wheels of administration. Ethnologists are calling for an 'end' to ethnology as a specialized field of knowledge. Economists are taking a critical look at the present crisis and trying to break with academic economics as well as with the 'applied' economics of the technocrats. The judges of the Magistrates' Union in France have challenged prevailing patterns of legal thinking on such issues as, for example, employers' responsibility for industrial accidents. The same basic problem crops up in a different way in each of these areas — the problem of defining a new relationship between political action and the intellectual knowledge which, because of its ideological implications, is an essential aspect of such action.

While taking into account all these struggles and debates, this book is also marked by my own recent and earlier experiences. Since childhood, we have been taught that it is wicked to say 'I', and this deeply rooted attitude is not easy to shake off. While working on this book, I tried to evaluate the original contribution of Marc Bloch in comparison with other French writings on the meaning of history, and was struck by the ease with which he used the first person singular in his *Apologie pour l'Histoire*. It immediately occurred to me that, influenced as I was by the conventional attitude of historians, I had remained silent about everything in my personal experience that had sharpened my sensitivity and given direction to my thinking.

■ *China and Vietnam* — which figure prominently in this book — were for many years my special field of study, the basis of my 'career'. But they were also a field of political activity through my participation in the various movements of solidarity with these two peoples. Not to speak of an extremely strong emotional bond, undoubtedly based on a deep and instinctive rejection of everything that bourgeois society, 'Christian civilization', 'Western culture', and 'modern' technique had forced on me since childhood. When I ceased to accept the academic historians' rhetoric, I also renounced my role as a 'specialist' on the contemporary history of these countries. The break was facilitated by the fact that China — and possibly Vietnam — had already broken completely with the academic history Establishment. These peoples are intensely alive to their relationship with the past but they are not interested in producing treatises 'of international standing', shining in the seminars and conferences of the West or seeing their names in the Table of Contents of the specialized orientalist reviews of the capitalist world. A word of warning here to those who still look in that direction for confirmation of the 'quality' of historical work in the new states of Africa or Asia. The revolutionary struggle of the Chinese, the Vietnamese or the Cambodians constitutes an active criticism of the Western historian's usual rhetoric, a stinging rejection of many a scholarly 'work', of many a 'successful' academic career. That revolutionary struggle fully exposes their futility.

■ *Long trips* and everything they represent for the privileged who have the opportunity to take advantage of them. In the course of my academic career, a skilful use of personal contacts and institutional possibilities enabled me, like many others, to make several trips to China and Vietnam, the Soviet Union and the United States, Australia and Madagascar. Such trips produce the effect of an almost physical contact with the planet in its totality. They have contributed enormously to my interest in comparative reflection on history as mankind's common past and the foundation of its common future – although the new internationalism has still to be defined.

■ *The Communist Party*, in which I spent twenty-one years of my life. The full story of its contribution and its trauma will some day have to be told. But that would necessitate rising above the emotional bitterness nearly all former members, especially intellectuals, feel towards the Party. The Communist Party is a political fact of life in contemporary France. At times it is a distinct annoyance to the Establishment. It enjoys the confidence of a large proportion of both the working class and the middle classes. And yet many of us take little interest in it, for the Party itself takes little interest in the grass-roots struggles that other sections of the working class and of the radicalized middle classes are now vigorously waging. 'Wild-cat' actions in the factories; the critique of the academic concept of personal advancement through individually acquired knowledge; the new thinking on the political content of delinquency; the critique of sexism and its stronghold, the army; the hatred of tyrannical foremen and of the élitist attitude of managers and experts – these currents cannot be attributed to a handful of leftist intellectuals manipulated by the power structure. They are the living experience of millions who do not identify with the Communist Party. As Georges Séguy, the Communist leader of the main French trade-union federation, quite logically and frankly put it: 'Society needs foremen as much as it does doctors or schoolteachers.' But it apparently has no use either for 'barefoot doctors', for 'open-door' universities, or for revolutionary shop-committees.

By its refusal to criticize the dominant ideology, academic Marxism has accepted the prevailing intellectualist, productivist, technicist rhetoric in the field of historical knowledge. By the same token, it has agreed to play the game of the academic system, with its honours and attractions. If the point is made several times in this book, it is because such conformism is a relatively recent development.

In the early 1950s, I lived through the sharp turn that led the French Communist Party to orient its intellectuals towards the institutions and outlook of the Establishment – it was then that the Party rejected Zhdanov's thesis concerning 'bourgeois science' and 'proletarian science'. Until then, French Communist intellectuals had systematically turned their backs on the poisoned delights of an academic career, following the example of such militant Communist Party writers as Politzer and Jacques Decour, who died in the struggle against Nazism after years of obscure activity in working-class organizations.

In the aftermath of May '68, I took my distance from both the Communist Party and the history Establishment. The process was a gradual one, free of painful conflicts — so natural that today I can hardly describe it, although it was accompanied by a deep personal crisis. It is no easy task to explain how I could have accepted, for so many years, the double conditioning of 'Party' and 'career'.

For I know only too well the *games of the mandarins*, their rewards in terms of money and prestige. I know what I am talking about when it comes to analysing the little world of the historians and its mechanisms. Is breaking — at least partially — with that system merely the ultimate phase in the career of a mandarin who remains privileged in his very non-conformism? Certainly — for my position as a university professor with tenure gives me genuine autonomy, genuine security, in the framework of the existing system. But those who point reproachfully to the privileges I still enjoy while rebelling against the Establishment have never answered the simple question: Why do so few of my 'peers' use their privileges in the same way as I do? And, after all, have I 'broken' in any real sense? My situation is one of comfortable autonomy rather than frugal independence. Like so many other intellectuals, I remain a prisoner of the system. But what is the point of personal flight? So many attempts at it have ended in pitiful failure. So I continue to perform my teaching duties and to pocket the tidy little sums to which I an 'entitled'. At the same time, I try to give my students something different from the tasteless fare that usually passes for historical knowledge.

As for May '68, it meant a great deal to many of us. It is no accident that the cynical expression — 'Sixty-eighters' — has become fashionable under the reign of President Giscard d'Estaing's 'advanced liberalism'. The dangers of creating a myth around 'May '68' are obvious — the Establishment itself stands to profit by it, for it can use an injection of new blood, of new ideas, of previously neglected talents, to give substance to the reforms it feels are unavoidable. Repentent 'Sixty-eighters' who have found their niche in the official Environment agencies, in sociological marketing, industrial counselling, cultural administration, advertising, etc., are innumerable. Like the 'Forty-eighters' and sobered followers of Saint-Simon, who offered their services to the commercial ventures of the Second Empire around 1850—60. But the 'beautiful month of May' deserves a better fate. Must we drift then into a backwards-looking mythology or the nostalgia of war veterans? No. May '68 can be evaluated as a *breach* and as a *phase*. It can be studied in its historical perspective for what it began and for what it expressed. In order to go further.

The ideas of this book were ruminated for years both in the solitude of my study and in common with my students in our seminars and workshops. But in France the critique of conventional history received a considerable boost recently through the activity of the 'History Forum', a movement of historians and non-historians interested in approaching his-

tory in a spirit of radical social criticism. While this book is a personal
contribution for which the Forum cannot be held responsible, it is deeply
indebted to the Forum's collective quest and has benefited enormously
from the exchanges of ideas the Forum made possible. Thanks to the
Forum, I was able to practise the historian's trade — at least occasionally
— outside the walls of the university. I take this opportunity to thank
all those whose suggestions and ideas have enriched the text — those who
reread the manuscript or simply provided ideas and information, whether
in classroom discussions or in friendly conversations somewhere in
Brittany or Occitania.*

Generally speaking, reflection, analysis and the development of ideas are
individual efforts in appearance only. Despite a writer's illusions about his
'creative freedom', every text has its roots in a given society, a given social
environment or political movement. Such being the case, why sign this
book?

Signing a book seems natural enough. The reader can give it a label,
the novice can 'make a name for himself', the publisher can profit from an
author's reputation. In any case, the individualistic morality of Western
capitalism requires the writer to assume personal responsibility for his
work. The elementary commercial principle — 'honour your signature' —
applies equally to intellectuals.

As if any work, this one included, were the author's brainchild exclusively! As if the information presented here, the analysis, the questions
raised, were conceived in the splendid isolation of his study! The writer is
but a relay, his work but a *reflection*. A book can do no more than help
define problems, enable them to mature — and that is the aim of this one.
But its facts, its analyses, its questions, could never have been articulated
if they had not already been in the air, circulating confusedly, present in
the collective consciousness because they are the *product of social experience* — in this case, the crisis of conventional history, among its producers
and its consumers alike. If we define history as an active, collective relationship to the past, historical deliberation can only be active and collective.
Individual contributions have a meaning only as so many attempts to
clarify and strengthen dynamic relationships of that type.

A signature, in any case, is an individualistic gesture. It derives from the
widespread taste for the limelight — consider the feverish excitement of
most authors in correcting their proofs, collecting reviews about their

* For the last fifteen years in the south of France — from Gascony to Provence — a
movement of reawakening has taken place, challenging the so-called 'colonial' control
of Paris centralism in terms of language, culture and economic development, and
pleading for another type of relationship with the central government. Geographic-
ally it comprises almost the whole southern third of the country; the protagonists
of the movement have named that area Occitania, although it was never in the past
a consistent political unit.

work, signing sample copies, not to mention pocketing their royalties. We love to attract attention to ourselves and our work — for that is what counts in the social competition of Western capitalism. Few authors can resist the pleasure of seeing their photos spread over the cover of their latest work! Perhaps the use of a pseudonym is the best protection against this more or less shamefaced exhibitionism. After all, Marx did not sign the *Communist Manifesto*, his 'best text' (to use the language of the more sophisticated critics), for his intention was precisely to serve as a relay and a reflection. He wanted to help the revolutionary workers of the League of the Just to develop their ideas and their perspectives — *and that is all.* The young left-wing intellectuals who founded the Chinese Communist Party during the 1920 and '30s used pseudonyms consistently — not so much for security reasons as to counteract bourgeois individualism. It seems that Qu Qiu-bai, the literary critic who was at one time General Secretary of the Chinese Communist Party and who was assassinated by the Guomindang in 1933, used fifty-three different pseudonyms in the course of his life. The left-wing scientists of the journal *Impascience* remain anonymous — not a single article is signed.

So much for the dangers of the signature from the author's side. From the side of the reader, we encounter the same ambiguities. The reader thinks he knows the author, his brand image, his record. He reads his latest work with reference to the idea he already has of him, his outlook and intentions. 'What's he doing now?' the reader asks, and looks into the files, so to speak, to find embarrassing twenty-year-old quotations — there is a touch of the policeman in many a critic.

The signature, moreover, has considerable publicity value in the mundane world of the spectator society. Political literature also has its stars and everyone pretends to have read the latest Marcuse or the latest Althusser. Once a person is familiar with the author's label and brand image, he can easily chat about a book he has read superficially — or not at all. But when the wrapping of individualized publicity is absent, the reader can judge a book only for its content and intrinsic value; he would never even bring the subject up unless he had really read it for himself.

Must we conclude that the best solution is the use of a pseudonym or mere anonymity if a work is to be spared this extra load of dross and irrelevancy both at the source (the author) and at the outlet (the reader), and so be enabled to play its double role as a reflection of social practice and a contribution to that practice?

After much hesitation, I finally decided to sign this book, since any writing — inevitably personal in form under present conditions — is, to a great extent, the product of the individual's life-experience, of all the writer-witness has suffered, loved, rejected, despised, believed. To sign this book means making the effort to say 'I' — and it is not always easy.

It is not our habit, and an outstanding scholar like Bloch could do it only after an intense crisis in his university career. This book is obviously a work of self-criticism. By taking responsibility for it and 'signing' it, I identify — proudly or regretfully — with the personal background that led up to it. But assuming responsibility need not imply self-centred narcissism. Personal confessions — by people who have 'succeeded', and by those whom the system has nearly crushed — are fashionable in the French publishing market of the 1970s. But such 'self questioning' is completely innocuous so long as it stops there. And besides, intellectuals enjoy talking about themselves once the ice is broken. But how can we go further and convert an innocuous confession into a political force?

This book's unfinished state is appropriate to its subject-matter. The reflection turns round and round, the threads weave and interlace, the same basic themes are approached from various angles: the Stalinist theory of the 'five stages', the historical significance of the Occitan movement, the critique of academic Marxism, the complex record of the Chinese experience. This winding, bushy path of thought is the expression of my own uncertainties.

But history is much too important a matter to be left to the historians.

1 History as a dynamic relationship to the past

Specialized 'field' or collective memory – the 'hunger for history' – on which side is historical knowledge? – the traps of intellectualism and professionalism – a spurious expansion

Many historians live in a state of complacent professionalism. History is their 'trade',* their 'field'.** They are specialists and respected as such. The press, and even more television, have familiarized the general public with their position as privileged experts on the past. This professional complacency is rooted in the ambiguity of the very word 'history', signifying both the underlying movement of events in time and the study of it. The subject-matter of biology is life, of astronomy the stars. But the subject-matter of history is – 'history'. This semantic identification is the sign both of extraordinary smugness and of a fatal trap.

Yet we feel that history is something quite different, that it concerns us all. Everyday language is replete with references to history. There is the 'wheel of history' that turns inexorably, but also stops, accelerates, changes direction. There are the 'ironies' of history, its 'tricks', its 'pit-falls', its 'designs', even its 'hidden side' for the Peeping Toms. History, it seems, is a vast self-adjusting machine capable of 'retaining' or 'forgetting' people, dates, facts. It even has its 'garbage-cans', for it is well organized. It can give 'lessons', confer laurels on those who perform on its 'stage', or even pronounce 'judgments' from the height of its 'tribunal' – and sometimes it keeps its 'secrets' and refuses to talk.

Behind these threadbare clichés is a message that is both coherent and dangerous: no less dangerous than the historian's claim to a monopoly of history. Namely, the idea that history is an outside force, dominating man by means of an authority derived from an irrevocable Past which leaves no alternative but submission. It is thus the past that rules the present.

*M. Bloch, *Apologie pour l'histoire ou le métier d'historien.*
**E. Le Roy Ladurie, *Le Territoire de l'historien.*

And yet, as Marx put it, 'History does nothing, it possesses no colossal riches, it fights no fights. It is rather *man,* real, living man who acts, possesses and fights . . .'*

The past has value only through what it means to us. It is the product of our collective memory and constitutes its essential tissue. This is true for what people have passively suffered – Verdun, the Great Depression of the 1930s, the Nazi Occupation, Hiroshima – as well as for what they have actively lived: e.g. in France, the Popular Front, the Resistance, May '68. But this past – recent or remote – has a meaning for us. It helps us understand the society in which we live; it enables us to know what is worth defending and preserving in it, what should be overthrown or destroyed. History is an *active* relationship to the past. The past is present in every field of social experience. The specialized work of the professional historians is an aspect of this collective and contradictory relationship of our society to its past – but an aspect only, and by no means the most significant one, nor one that is independent of the social context and the prevailing ideology.

The collective relationship of society to its past, the active knowledge of the past, is experienced both as *constraint* and *need.* The past weighs on us and we strive to break its hold. 'Make a clean slate of the past!' – these words from the *Internationale* still strike a chord.

At the same time, 'there exists a deep hunger for history among the people', according to the contemporary French 'amateur' historian, Claude Manceron. 'When the present is hard to bear, ancestors are always needed', wrote *Le Monde* (26 July 1974), commenting on the simultaneous publication of a book on the Gauls and another on the American cowboys.

It is true that this 'hunger for history' can be an urgent, elemental demand – a search for asylum from the pain of the present. But it can also become a will to struggle, a pivot for action. The stake of Montségur – where the last partisans of the heretical sect of Cathars in southern France were exterminated in 1224 – is intensely alive in the consciousness of the reawakening Occitan movement, as is the memory of the slave-trade in the Black Power movement in the United States . . . leaving aside, for the moment, the uncertainties and ambiguities of these two social movements.

History – our common past – is everyone's affair. A few professional historians have sensed this and tried to provide a more collective, less technical and specialized, definition of history and historical science.

Take J. Burckhardt's, for example: 'The record of what one age finds worthy of note in another', or that of Lucien Febvre: 'It is the

*K. Marx, *The Holy Family.*

need felt by every human group at each phase of its development to seek out and emphasize those facts, events, trends of the past that prepare for the present, that enable us to understand and live it.'

In one respect, these historians of an earlier generation were far more modest than the computer technocrats of today: they were willing to put their ear to the ground and listen to what the people of their age were saying. That they remained pure intellectuals, however, is indicated by such phrases as 'find worthy of note in the past', 'understand' the present, etc. For them, the intellectual grasp of the past, even when viewed as a collective experience, was an end in itself, whether or not it led to some form of *social practice,* to an active and concrete commitment.

Yet our knowledge of the past is a dynamic factor in the development of society, a significant stake in the political and ideological struggles of today, a sharply contested area. What we know of the past can be of service either to the Establishment or to the people's movement. History is linked to the class struggle. It is never neutral — never above the battle. The militant Occitan singer, Claude Marti, glorifies the rebellious wine-growers of 1907 and the draft-resisters of Languedoc who refused in 1811 to make war and die for Napoleon in Germany or Russia. On the other hand, the memory of Joan of Arc and the anniversary of her adventure are regularly exploited by the forces of right-wing nationalism and conservative Catholicism.

On which side is historical knowledge today? Whose interests are served by the dynamic relationship between the past and the present? That is a question no historian can evade — however much he may want to do so.

In viewing society's relationship to its past as the basis of historical knowledge, the traditional relationship between the past and the present is reversed. It is no longer the past that rules and passes judgment. It is the present that defines the issues and makes demands.

But the present needs the past only with reference to the future. The problem is not merely to 'live the present better' as Lucien Febvre would have it, but to change (or defend) it. In the last analysis, collective memory, the appeal to history, has meaning only in terms of what is to come. The dialectical relationship between past and future — a combination of unity and struggle, of continuity and change — is the very fabric of history. As Mao Ze-dong put it:

> The history of mankind is one of continuous development from the realm of necessity to the realm of freedom. This process is never-ending. In any society in which classes exist class struggle will never end. In classless society the struggle between the new and the old and between truth and falsehood will never end . . . . Therefore, man

has constantly to sum up experience and go on discovering, inventing, creating and advancing.*

In emphasizing the active, collective character of historical knowledge, of the relationship to the past, we de-emphasize the conventional themes of the historian's rhetoric and the false assumptions that are so widely accepted few even bother to challenge them:

■ *Intellectualism:* The intellectual understanding of the past is regarded as a worthwhile end in itself, independently of actual social experience. The historians have ingeniously invented the distinction between 'making history' and 'writing history'. The former is the domain of 'politicians' with the occasional intervention — welcome or regrettable, depending on whether the viewpoint is left or right — of the people. The latter is the domain reserved for historians.

But such intellectualism is deeply rooted. The professional historians take it for granted and the general public accepts it. Marc Bloch, for example, wrote his *Apologie pour l'histoire* when he was driven from the Sorbonne, hunted by the Nazis and on his way to the underground resistance, torture and death. Yet he resorts to the language of the academic aristocracy:

'History must be eternally indifferent to *homo faber* and *homo politicus* and no more need be said in its defence than that is is indispensable to the development of *homo sapiens*. History has aesthetic delights of its own.'

■ *Apolitical objectivism:* 'A good historian belongs to no time and no country.' This phrase of Fénelon's evokes a disdainful smile whenever it is quoted as being hopelessly old-fashioned. Yet as recently as 1968, Paul Veyne, a highly respected specialist in ancient history, could still write in that contemporary French compendium of human knowledge, the *Encyclopedia Universalis,* under the entry 'History':

'A serious — in other words, disinterested — historian does not study the history of France because he happens to be French. He does so out of love for history.'

Few professional historians are willing to reflect seriously and rigorously on the role of their work in a country's social and political life. Does it benefit the Establishment or the revolutionary struggle? Few care to think about the relationship between the subjects they choose to study — even the way their studies are carried on — and the stability of the existing system. They live comfortably with the concept of an airtight separation between their 'craft' and the larger society.

■ *Professionalism:* History, the knowledge of the past, is regarded as a

*Quotations from Chairman Mao Tse-Tung ('Little Red Book'), p. 203.

function of the technical qualifications and know-how of the professional historian. Historical knowledge is supposedly manufactured in the splendid isolation of the historian's laboratory. The product of his specialized research is then treated at descending levels and finally distributed to the consuming public in the form of textbooks, 'amateur' history, works of popularization, etc.

The rejection of this élitist rhetoric does not imply the evasion of certain real and difficult problems: Can specialization be dispensed with in the effort to understand the past? Is it possible to criticize historical professionalism while at the same time insisting on scientific 'accuracy'? Historians usually discuss such issues only within the closed circle of their profession and look upon its privileged status as natural. Yet the specific problems of the historian's craft can be approached effectively only when he has succeeded in repudiating the conventional role of the past and its usual place in a society such as ours that is divided against itself and torn by sharp social conflicts.

The output of the historian's profession is currently expanding and many professionals applaud the fact. We have hundreds of theses, a proliferation of specialized journals, innumerable works for the general public, scholarly conferences on a wide variety of subjects, the frequent reprinting of ancient documents and other profitable publishing ventures. But this spectacular expansion conceals the need for a political discussion around the question: What is the meaning of all this activity and whose interests does it serve?

The old-fashioned history of events has lost none of its vigour but two new currents among French historians are on the rise in the media and television especially. First, the 'New History' best exemplified by the collective works of Pierre Nora and Jacques Le Goff (*Faire de l'Histoire*, Paris 1973, 3 vols). This school strives to exert an influence on the general public through the media; it makes an effort to be attractive, open to human problems, to varied ways of thinking, to life-and-death issues. Second, the universalist Marxist history based on the prestige and material means of academic Soviet history as well as on the positions won by the French Communist Party in the academic Establishment since 1968 — new departments, scholarly journals, conferences, etc. Both these currents, engaged in a complex play of rivalry and cooperation, accept the false assumptions of the historian's rhetoric and the rules and regulations that govern the practice of history in the university world. Both schools — whose impact we shall emphasize again and again in subsequent chapters — propagate a conception of historical mechanisms based on *gradualism,* on processes external to the *active* movement of masses of people. For the first group, the underlying thread is the 'long-range view' popularized in France by Professor Fernand Braudel; for the second, it is the concept of productive forces slowly but inexorably entering into conflict with the relations of production, as Louis Althusser learnedly explained in his polemic against the British Marxist philosopher John Lewis. The result in both cases is to remove history from the possession of the people, to drive them from the historical field by restricting the study of history to privileged specialists and casting doubt on their capacity to intervene actively to 'make history'. What the practitioners of the 'New History' and the Marxist academics have in common with each other and with the old-fashioned 'history of events' is the inability to recognize the basic relationship between historical knowledge and social practice.

2 History and social practice: in the Establishment camp

The past as a source of political power – official anniversaries – the control of sources and occultation – Gaullism and Giscardism: attitudes toward the French past – who is disturbed by the past? – every class society has its own way of controlling the past

In class societies, history is one of the tools the ruling class uses to maintain its power. The state apparatus tries to *control the past* at the level of both political action and ideology.

The state and the power structure organize the past and build its image in terms of their own political and ideological interests. In the ancient Egypt of the Pharaohs, or in feudal China, time was reckoned by the succession of dynasties that marked the periods of history and gave substance to the society's historical consciousness. Written by official committees of scribes or mandarins, history was a state service that defined the power structure of the monarchy as the basis of the social order throughout historical time. This was also the structure and function of French history up to the nineteenth century; it was laid out in terms of the succession of royal clans, and the names of the Merovingian, Carolingian and Capetian rulers – together with the ideology underlying the concept of monarchy – were early impressed upon the minds of children. If the historical rhetoric of the rising bourgeoisie seems more liberal and its approach more universal, that is because 'Ancient Times' and the 'Middle Ages' provide an excellent foil for 'Modern Times', which brings the rule of the bourgeoisie to fruition and opens the future to its power. The French historians of the nineteenth century – like Tocqueville, Duruy, Lavisse, Seignobos – were ideologically consistent. For them, 'progress' culminated in the specific power of the rising class and guaranteed its continuity.

Ruling classes and governments frequently appeal to the past explicitly. Tradition (even in its specific cultural aspects), continuity, history – all are invoked as justification for their domination. In Bossuet's view, the absolute monarchy of the Very Christian King was the culmination of world history from the early wanderings of the Jews to the Christian era. According to Hegel, the Prussian state was the preeminent product of the dialectic of history. Tchang Kai-chek's Guomindang openly identified with the traditionalism of Confucius and fought Communism in the name of the Chinese past. The appeal to the 'authority' of the past has the same function in the reactionary philosophy of the French monarchists of 1815, such as De Bonald, as in the hands of contemporary Moslem conservatives.

Closer to home, the political power of Gaullism was based – among other things – on a skilful appropriation of the 'French past', viewed as the common possession of the people. Words like permanence, continuity, tradition, heritage, constantly recurred in the Gaullist historical rhetoric with the aim of strengthening the authority and prestige of the General. His 'France' was an absolute, an all-powerful idea demanding unlimited sacrifice and unquestioning obedience. De Gaulle was supposedly the receptacle and continuator of what he called 'a certain idea of France'.

De Gaulle himself described in these words his resignation from the government in 1946: 'The General took away with him something fundamental, permanent, necessary, that he incarnated by historical right and that the regime of Parties could not represent.'

On Armistice Day, 11 November 1968, he spoke as if he were trying to exorcise the demon of May '68:

> The fatherland remembers . . . The same flame a generation earlier aroused the entire country, later caused it to build monuments to the dead in our villages and cities, and on each November 11 assembles the people around the flags of our war veterans; it burns symbolically beneath the Arch of Triumph at the Etoile. . . . The same flame will inspire the soul of eternal France throughout the future as it has throughout the past.

At times, the use of the past is not so direct, not so explicit. It is with the help of a diffuse ideology that history is called to the defence of the power structure and the interests of the ruling class, through textbooks, films, television, pictures, etc. For example, the schoolbook portrayal of Louis XIV is anything but innocent. The 'great man' is the master of history, yesterday and today as well. His setbacks are seen as the result of his 'faults', and the mind of the child is thus educated to moralistic breast-beating. Civil war is invariably presented in a negative light, in contrast with foreign wars, those moments of sacrifice, of heroism and glory. Civil war is the supreme catastrophe: Armagnacs against Burgundians, the wars of religion, the Commune of 1871. The vivid coloured prints produced in the town of Epinal in the nineteenth century were most effective in propagating an historical ideology among the largely illiterate French masses.

The characteristic themes were the prestige of the army and rulers, family morality, the redeeming value of work. The same point can be made for the 'retro' fashion in the French films of the early 1970s. It accurately mirrored the political mechanisms by which the Pompidou clique intended to hold power: The films about the 'gay nineties', the 'mad twenties', about the Vichy period particularly — all were marked by political cynicism, the spirit of individualism, the deliberate avoidance of current problems.

Sometimes the state apparatus intervenes more directly to ritualize the past and twist the collective memory to its own purposes. This occurs on the occasion of national holidays, solemn commemorations and anniversaries. November 11 is highly political: it was in 1919 that in France the date of the 1918 Armistice was designated as a premier national holiday in an atmosphere of jingoistic fervour and sentimental demagogy about the war veterans. In 1970, the Persepolis Festival served the interests of the absolute monarchy in Iran by reinforcing its power inside the country while contributing to its integration into the 'modern' world of multinational capitalism. In 1976, the celebration of the Bicentennial of American Independence was marked by numerous scholarly seminars and historical spectacles, by official speeches and commercial gadgets, the publication of luxuriously bound documents of the period, the visits of schoolchildren to the landmarks of the Revolution. The purpose of such activity was to impress the American people with the old idea of their 'manifest destiny' — to remind them that they had always been on the side of justice and righteousness, as long as they remained united and respectful of their leaders. The virulent class conflicts that marked the era of the War of American Independence were carefully brushed aside, as was the racist behaviour of the 'young Democracy' towards the Indians, whose genocide was essential to its development.

All these anniversaries and commemorations — one could add Churchill's funeral, the Bicentennial of Cook's arrival in Australia, the Centennial of the Meiji in the conservative Japan of 1968 — have certain features in common: the official sponsorship of an historical celebration; a mass spectacle with popular festivities; the stereotyped portrayal of a past event to fortify the ideology of the existing power structure; the occultation of the non-official aspects of the event, such as social conflicts and mass struggles.

The central power uses the past in a still more direct and active way: its political behaviour and decisions, its options, are based on an investigation of the past, especially the recent past, conducted by its police, its research bureaux, its administrative services, etc. The state's brand of 'histoire immédiate'* is a secret operation with respect to both the collection of material and the interpretation of it. Its investigations are carried out for the state's purposes exclusively and with an efficiency that is occasionally revealed to those concerned when, for example, documents come to light following a war, a revolution or a scandal. Such practical history, directly based on the past–present relationship, is infinitely more operational than many a scholarly discourse by professional historians.

The state power structure also supervises the knowledge of the past at its source. The great majority of 'first-hand documents', so prized by historians, originate with the state or its adjuncts, and this is particularly true of quantified materials:

> The historian's territory is completely marked out by the apparatus of repression. . . . Our memory is that of the power structure which functions as a gigantic recording machine, using the official archives of Government services (Tax Offices, Treasury, etc.), church archives (ecclesiastical accounts, hospitals, parish records, etc.), the archives of powerful private interests (trusts, big commercial firms, etc.). We know nothing of reality except what can be inferred from the information the power structure has recorded and made available.**

The control the state exercises over the past and the collective memory at the 'source' often takes the form of withholding information. The archives keep certain facts secret and sometimes even destroy embarrassing material. As a result, entire sections of world history have no other existence than what the oppressors permit us to know of them. Chinese peasant revolts are known through the writings of the mandarin historians, the Carthaginians are known through the records of the Romans, the Albigenses through the accounts of royal or priestly chroniclers. Sometimes reality is distorted, sometimes it is suppressed completely. As an extreme example of this official logic, the Confucian mandarins referred to rebels and dissidents as *fei* — a negative grammatical expression denoting non-persons, those who *do not exist* in the eyes of history.

Occultation is one of the most widespread practices in the state's system of control over the past. The past is a nuisance to be gotten rid of. In the aftermath of the American debacle in Indochina in 1975, Henry Kissinger urged the American people not to waste time debating

---

*A special interest is developing in France for 'histoire immédiate', namely, for the immediate past as a field open to the professional historian, in reaction to the old idea that the historian can only study properly those periods which he could view 'from a distance'.

**L'Idéal historique', *Recherches*, 14.

the past but to face the future in a spirit of national unity. And Mike Mansfield, leader of the Democratic 'opposition' in the Senate at the time, said he agreed with the President that recriminations over recent history were out of place.

Imperialist and colonial wars are a favourite area for this type of reductionist operation. In France, for example, the Resistance is now blandly presented as a romantic non-political episode of the country's recent experience without the slightest class content. But the Algerian war! The subject is tabu in the eyes of French government and ruling-class circles who are now involved with Algiers in a neo-colonial policy that could only be embarrassed by an analysis of its origins. The subject is also tabu for the French people, who prefer to forget their own collective responsibility for the repression and tortures of a war waged against an entire nation. The Algerian war is also tabu for the principal organizations of the French labour movement. For them, that war — like the First World War — was the 'moment of truth', the proof of their inability to put their internationalist principles into practice. In Algeria itself, the situation is no different. A national committee for historical research was recently set up there for the purpose of collecting all the documents and relics relating to the war of liberation. It was headed by the security chief and its real aim was to put safely out of the way any material or testimony that might prove 'embarrassing' to certain elements. The Algerian people responded massively to the appeal to cooperate with the newly-created committee — and subsequently heard nothing more about it. Once again, the collective memory was dispossessed.

An analysis of the power structure's *occultation* of the past makes possible a comparison between the historical rhetoric of Gaullism and that of the current President of the French Republic, Giscard d'Estaing. Here we encounter a revealing test of the difference between two political strategies of the French bourgeoisie. When Giscard abolished the celebration of 8 May, anniversary of the 1945 victory of the Allies over the Nazis and a high-point of Gaullist mythology, he declared, 'That war was fratricidal for Europe. It is the common aspiration of our two peoples that it be the last. . . . To mark this certitude, I have decided to commemorate this anniversary no longer. It is time to look to the future.'

Under Giscard d'Estaing, the ruling circles thus embraced the ideology of 'modernism' that was already systematically cultivated for some time by the American-style supercapitalism which the French bourgeoisie found repugnant under De Gaulle ('Continue France!' was their motto) and accepted only with the greatest reluctance under Pompidou and the group around him. 'Let us glorify modernism,' they said in effect, 'but at the same time let us respect the traditions of the soil and the people.' With Giscard d'Estaing, the decisive step was taken. In line with the ideology of United States capitalism, the American political conscience is defined as 'a-historical' (an obvious oversimplification); in similar fashion, Giscard d'Estaing and his government are trying to place France in a state of 'historical weightlessness'. 'Live in the present,' they say. 'The past does not interest us.' In this way, the historical reference-points that make possible a radical critique of the present — and the definition of a qualitatively different future — are lost sight of. Capitalism identifies itself with only one possible future — its own. The past, of course, has disappeared neither from official rhetoric nor from the social environment, but it is no longer the glorified sovereign that De Gaulle so forcefully evoked. Now the past is cut to measure, reduced to the disparate elements of an innocuous system. It can still, naturally, be manipulated for the official needs of the moment — for example, a presidential speech on the anniversary of Joan of Arc, the use of 'Old French' symbols to identify a massive concrete housing project in the suburbs of Paris, or the President's alleged family tree connecting him with the French monarchs of the eighteenth century.

The occultation of the past is a favourite practice of the power structure. But is it a monopoly of the Western ruling classes? China and the Soviet Union offer numerous examples of official silence concerning delicate episodes in their own history or controversial figures like Trotsky or Lin Piao. The past is an embarrassment to those whose concern it is to preserve their own power — regardless of its political label — within a Party or state apparatus. But should every attempt to discard the past be equally condemned? Who feels threatened by the past? What are the priorities and criteria? Where can the line be drawn between the *selective* clarification of the past in terms of genuine struggles or real political priorities on the one hand, and outright occultation, the falsification of history for reasons of state, on the other? Every political choice involves a risk of error.

It would be out of the question to criticize the Vietnamese revolutionaries for calling on the population to forget the divisions of the recent past and concentrate their efforts on the reconstruction of the country after the liberation of Saigon in April 1975. In that case, the past — people's attitudes towards the revolutionary struggle and towards the American puppet regime until the day of liberation — might well interfere with the common task of reconstruction which currently takes priority. But when is such reasoning really based on the aspirations and interests of the people? And when is it only manipulatory rhetoric?

The control of the past by the power structure is a phenomenon common to all class societies, but it is carried out through specific tech-

niques in accordance with the demands of each prevailing mode of
production. In the Asian societies, for example, history was an affair of
state, a basic responsibility and essential prop of each dynasty. Under
the feudal system in Western Europe, history was an extension of the
prevalent moralistic and religious rhetoric of medieval Christianity; it
served as an illustration of Christian morality, of the belief in divine
omnipotence and the authority of the monarchy and the landowners. In
the Soviet Union, where the social structure is apparently quite different,
the relationship is no less specific. The 'five-stage theory' — first propounded during the Stalinist era — offers a general pattern for world
history: primitive communism, slavery, feudalism, capitalism, socialism.
The power structure of the Soviet bureaucracy is seen as the culmination of human history, its legitimacy as established once and for all.
The use of history is one of the defence mechanisms of the new privileged
stratum. In China, where the situation is much more complex — there is
open talk of a 'struggle between two lines' — a contradiction exists
between a grass-roots history directly experienced by the masses of
people, and an authoritarian, dogmatic approach. On the one hand, there
is an appeal to the collective memory of the people, while on the other,
the entire previous career of Liu Shao-Qi is distorted beyond recogni-
tion when the crisis breaks out, and the Lin Piao affair is cloaked in
official silence, with only belated and fragmentary versions reaching the
public, at least abroad.

During the era of liberal capitalism, there is a specific relationship
between the demands of the prevailing mode of production and the
political function of historical knowledge. This relationship is not, however, direct or mechanical. It consists both of open intervention by the
state — as in the above-mentioned examples — and of diffuse ideological
pressure. The historians are convinced that they enjoy 'freedom of
expression', but in their professional work they exhibit behaviour which
is characteristic of capitalist society as a whole.

Conventional historians, with their pose of objectivity, pretend to be
unaware that they are reinforcing the power of an institution or a
political apparatus by conferring upon it the authority of the past. An
obvious example is the history of the Roman Catholic Church, an ideological system that inculcates such values as stability, continuity,
gradualism. Left-wing Christians answer by emphasizing the reality of
the Catholic past with its crises, uncertainties, schisms, desertions,
conflicts. The same remarks apply to the development of the French
educational system as French historians like Durkheim, Marrou or
Prost write it. They present it as an example of uninterrupted progress
from the days of Charlemagne, legendary founder of schools, to the
compulsory primary education of the Third Republic, with the Jesuit

Colleges and the Napoleonic lycées among its significant landmarks. This ideological rhetoric is historical only in form — its purpose is to portray as an absolute, an 'historic', reality the present system of educational confinement and ideological conditioning in terms of such capitalist attitudes as the passive respect for knowledge, individual competitiveness, the acceptance of social inequalities in the name of alleged inequalities of 'capacity' and 'aptitude'.

The real function of historiography (the history of history) should be to identify and describe the specific relationship between historical knowledge and the prevailing mode of production. Yet few professional historians take an interest in this task; they approach it, if at all, from a purely narrative point of view, simply tracing the progress of historical knowledge over the years through the accumulation of facts and the refinement of critical methods. History is viewed as an autonomous intellectual activity moving in a kind of closed circuit.

The fraternity of professional historians willingly adopt such 'colleagues' of the past as Thucydides and Ibn Khaldun, Froissart and Gibbon. These are the 'pioneers' they are fond of referring to, if only to convince themselves of the 'progress' that has been made. It is a fact that the ruling classes — operating, as always, through the specific relationships of each society — have nearly always confided the study of the past to professional or semi-professional historians: priests and monks, bureaucrats, archivists, retired politicians, the idle rich, teachers. This élitism is a constant. Genuine 'freelance' militant historians are very rare; one can think, for example, of Buonarotti, survivor of the 1796 Babeuf conspiracy, and subsequent biographer of Babeuf, or Lissagaray, survivor and historian of the Paris Commune. Otherwise, historical knowledge has been the monopoly of a minority working in collusion with the ruling classes, accepting their values and enjoying a similarly comfortable life — and this applies equally to the ancient Egyptian scribe, the Soviet academician, or the 'left-liberal' historian of the Western university world.

For the masses of people, however, the past is meaningful only at the opposite pole of social existence — where it becomes involved directly in their struggles.

3 History and social practice: on the side of the people's struggles

The past rejected or put to use – Québecois, Aborigines and Occitans – how national movements and social struggles are anchored in the past: the bourgeoisie and the people – the traps of a mythical past: scientific accuracy and political intransigence – 'Year 01' as a break in time

In the struggle against the existing order, there is a natural tendency to reject the past and its record of oppression. 'Make a clean slate of the past!' During the French Revolution, statues were decapitated, armouries demolished, genealogical records and feudal deeds burned. In China, the slogan of the Cultural Revolution was to sweep away the 'four olds': old ideas, old customs, old culture, old habits.

But the rejection of the past does not exclude recourse to the past. In opposition to the official version of the past – mutilated, distorted, censored in the interests of the power structure – the people develop a version that better corresponds to their own aspirations and reflects the *genuine* richness of their history.

This tendency was quite marked in the national liberation movements of Central Europe during the nineteenth century. The nationalists of Hungary, Bohemia, Serbia and Rumania published old texts, wrote books on their national history, collected fairy tales and medieval works of art; everything that brought out the value of their own past contributed to the struggle against the domination of Turkey or Austria.

This determination to liberate the past, to use it for the assertion of national identity, is equally strong in the liberation movements of the Third World today. The very names of the new states – Ghana, Mali, etc. – revive the traditions of the Black Middle Ages that had been completely forgotten during the colonial period when these countries were called the 'Gold Coast' or the 'French Sudan'. The revolutionary Tupamaros of Uruguay adopted and popularized the name of the last Inca prince (Tupa-Amaru) who resisted the Spaniards in the sixteenth century. Thus, the struggles of today are anchored in the past. The approach of the Vietnamese and Palestinian revolutionaries is the same – their military units and offensive armies bear the names of famous warriors and battles of the national past, such as Tran Hung Dao, who defeated the Mongols in the thirteenth century, or Yarmuk, the great victory of the Arabs over the Byzantines in the seventh century.

The reclamation, the reconquest, of the past often takes the form of a reversal of values and symbols — it can become an occasion for derision. When the Indian militants occupied the vacated island prison of Alcatraz in San Francisco Bay in 1970, they offered to pay the symbolic sum of twenty-four dollars — the price the whites offered the Indians for the island of Manhattan in the seventeenth century.

The preservation of historical sites is one of the demands of the people — the right to their own past is an aspect of the demand for the right to exist today, as a Cherokee Indian explained in his own style:

> When the Cherokee people moved up into Tennessee a couple of thousand years ago, they settled along the little Tennessee River. They built numerous homes and villages. The bulk of the whole Cherokee society started there. . . .
>
> Today there are very few Cherokee sites of old villages left. They have all been flooded or destroyed. The only area left which holds any history to the Cherokee that remains is along the Tennessee. Now it is being threatened to be flooded, too. The Government has plans for a dam. . . .
>
> There is no great need for genociding a people's history when the whole eastern part of Tennessee is dotted with lakes. . . . The Cherokee people have been run off their land, have been herded together like cattle and have been shipped to a foreign land and have been raped of their identity. Now the Government is going to complete the job by coming back and saying these same Indian people do not have any right to have a place where they can come and say to their grand-children: 'This is where our great village sites were. This is where our culture started. This is where we cultivated our language. This is where we started from.'
>
> The white man is taking this from us. This is where the white man is committing total genocide on a people.*

For the Aborigines of Australia, too, the affirmation of their own past is an aspect of their protest against white domination and against the virtual extermination of their people. They accuse the Australian history books of ignoring them and point out that they have been occupying the land since time immemorial, for tens of thousands of years, and that their traditional non-agricultural way of life is anything but 'primitive', for it is based on an extremely elaborate ecological and demographical balance: hunting and fishing to a certain extent, birth control, health control, etc. The white man's invasion brought the diseases that ravage them today and forced them into reserves on the pretext of converting them. The reaffirmation of this ancient past is accompanied by a political awakening. The Queen's procession, which took place there in 1970 to commemorate

Liberation News Service, 1 November 1972.

the arrival of Captain Cook under the insulting slogan 'Bicentennial of Australia', was attacked by demonstrators carrying black-lined banners with the names of the tribes exterminated by the whites. An 'Aboriginal Embassy' was inaugurated under a tent before the Parliament at Canberra.

In Quebec, too, the revision of official history is regarded as one of the essential points of departure for the people's struggles:

> Our élites have told us many tales about our past. They have never located our past in history. The stories they told us about our past were invented to keep us, the people of Quebec, outside the mainstream of history.
> The élite that collaborated with the English colonizer after the defeat of the rebellion of 1837–1838 was like every other élite of a colonized people. Instead of fighting to free Quebec of the colonizer, it concentrated on our 'historic' past so as to evade the realities of the present. It glorified the exploits of Champlain, of Madeleine of Vercheres, of the Holy Martyrs of Canada.
> Generations of Canadians were indoctrinated with a rear-guard nationalism that describes us as a chosen people with the mission of evangelizing the world and spreading the Catholic religion over the entire American continent. . . .
> We, the people of Quebec, are subjected to colonialism. We are an imprisoned people. To change our situation, we must first understand it. To understand it, we must analyze the historical forces that led up to it.
> This little text-book is intended as an act of repossession. The repossession of our history is the first step toward the repossession of ourselves, a precondition for the repossession of our future.*

Similarly, when the Occitan militants reject the official version of history – in other words, the history of a centralized France – they show their determination to take possession of their own past in order to re-examine it and assert their identity more effectively.

At the Montségur Assembly of June 1972, the young Occitans declared:

> We learn the history of France, that is to say, the history of the centralization process carried out by Louis XIV and Napoleon. But what we want is to rediscover the history of the peoples who constitute France. They hide from us the poetry of the troubadours, the administrative system of the medieval cities, the history of the Camisard peasants who fought against King Louis XIV, the rebellions of the winegrowers of Languedoc. . . . Our past has been stolen from us and today we are relearning our history at the point where it was interrupted.**

As the political demands of the Bretons, the Occitans, the Alsatians and the Corsicans against the centralism of Paris intensify, the accent is

* Léandre Bergeron, preface to the *Petit Manuel d'histoire du Québec*, Montreal 1972.
** *Le Monde*, 26 June 1972.

placed on the *grass-roots* content of their specific heritage. This means breaking with the apolitical conservatism of the medieval-styled Celtic bards and the poets (*'Félibres'*) who kept alive the regional dialect of Provence. In the course of a single year, 1975, the following cultural events took place in France: the Alsatian Cultural Front celebrated the Peasant's War of 1525; the Occitan theatre group 'La Carriera' performed a play about the strike of the Cevenol miners in the nineteenth century (it was called 'Tabo', meaning 'Hold on!' in the local dialect); the Occitan theatre of Toulon travelled all over the south putting on a play about the armed struggle in the southern French Alps against the 1851 *coup d'état* of Napoleon III; the Bretons commemorated the tricentennial of the revolt of the Red Bonnets of 1675 (the very title of the event represents a cultural reconquest, since the French textbooks invariably describe it from the police viewpoint as the 'Stamp Tax Revolt'). Today's struggles against French centralist capitalism are being anchored in these people's struggles of past centuries.

For social struggles are nourished by the past. The memory of the labour movement is filled with the recollection of strikes that were sometimes national in scope (like those of 1936, for example) but in other cases of merely local concern and completely forgotten elsewhere, although they left a deep mark on the region where they occurred. At Millau in the south of France, the big strike of the leather workers in 1935 belongs to the collective experience of the French working class. In Roger Vailland's novel, *Beau Masque*, the mobilizing power of the workers' memory is symbolized by the worker Cuvrot, a veteran of the 1925 strike in the spinning mills of the little valley of Bugey in the southern part of the French Juras, and organizer (in the book, that is) of the 1951 strikes against acceleration of production and the effects of the Marshall Plan.

In China, the appeal to the people's memory is systematically organized. Ballads and stories reflecting the tradition of peasant's struggles against oppression are carefully collected. During an ordinary tourist visit in 1974, I met at least a dozen old people who were in the habit of recounting their recollections of feudal domination, capitalist factories, the Japanese occupation, the tyranny of the Guomindang. There is a consistent policy of organizing communication between the generations. Memories of oppression and struggle emphasize the political capacities of the people, their ability to assume control of their own affairs, as was the case during the mass movement of the Great Leap Forward of the Cultural Revolution.

In the United States, too, the past is a stake in hard-fought political struggles. 'Revisionist' historians like W. A. Williams, Gabriel Kolko, David Horowitz, Harvey Goldberg contest the conventional version of

American history — the glorification of the supposedly egalitarian life
of the *frontier*, the concept of the *consensus*, the naive belief in Manifest
Destiny, the so-called mission of the United States throughout the world.
The 'revisionists' stress the reality of American imperialism and racism,
the spuriousness of formal democracy. They demolish the myth of the
'non-historical' American mentality — a myth that clears the way for the
capitalist ideology of *laissez faire* and expansionism. The dissident
historians of the university world are not the only ones to wage this
battle against American mythology — the role played by the country's
oppressed minorities is even more vigorous. The Indians point out that
American history did not begin with the arrival of the white man. The
Blacks demand the inclusion of African studies departments in the university curricula to counteract the conventional image of an America with
no other history than that of the whites. The Chicanos (Mexican-Americans)
and the Puerto Ricans assert their Hispanic cultural background as against
the dominant Anglo-Saxon one. The Cajuns of southern Louisiana cling
to the French language; as recently as June 1977 the International *Herald-
Tribune* reported publication of the first textbook for teaching the Cajun
language.

A knowledge of the past gives rise to both *nostalgia* and *wrath*, as the
English Romantics were fond of reminding their contemporaries. The same
point was made before them by Diderot in a letter to Voltaire:

'Other historians recount the facts for our information. You recount
them to arouse in our hearts an intense hatred of lies, of ignorance, of
hypocrisy, of superstition, of tyranny, and the anger remains even when
the memory of the facts has vanished.'

But examples also abound — and this is an even more complicated
problem — of idealization of the past to give a stronger foundation to
the people's struggles against the rich and powerful. In the seventeenth
century, the radical sect of the Levellers, in their fight against the British
bourgeois monarchy, drew from a naïve, idealized picture of the primitive
Saxon democracy that antedated the Norman Conquest their hatred of
the wealthy and the landlords. The Taipings of nineteenth-century China
based their struggle against Chinese feudalism and the domination of the
Manchus on an idealized conception of the Zhou dynasty (first millen-
nium before Christ), which they imagined as a kind of egalitarian agricultural society.

During the French Revolution, images and symbols from the Roman
Republic played a similar role: *e.g.* Roman, or rather pseudo-Roman,
costumes, first names ('Gracchus' Babeuf, etc.), the political vocabulary,
David's historical paintings. The bourgeoisie and their allies found in this
theatrical Romanism useful weapons against the Christian, royalist culture
of the *ancien régime* they were committed to destroy. What counted for

them was the political impact, not historical accuracy. They meant to show that the new society was legitimate, that it could assume responsibility for establishing a new order with claims to universality (the 'sister Republics' of the Directory, the golden age of French Revolutionary Romanism in 1795—99), since it could appeal to Republican precedents more ancient and more respectable than those of the French feudal monarchy.

The function of history in the social practice of the ruling classes was relatively easy to define. But the active relationship the people's struggles have established with their past is much more complicated — which accounts for the inventory-like descriptive character of the above examples: Quebec and the Indians of the USA, the Occitans and the Australian Aborigines, the national liberation struggles of the nineteenth century and the French workers' struggles against the employers. A theoretical clarification is needed — but that would take us beyond the limits of the present essay. Many questions arise and it is for those who participate in these struggles to answer them. Is it true that the past is more important for marginal, minority struggles than for the 'major' struggles? Does the past mean as much to the workers as to the peasants (remember the Taiping rebellion) or the artisans (the Levellers, for example)? When does recourse to the past merely help the bourgeoisie rally the masses to its side (as in the case of the national movements of nineteenth-century Europe) and when is it, on the contrary, a genuinely popular approach? How can historical myths widespread among the people be distinguished from those invented by the bourgeoisie for popular consumption?

These are questions that must be raised on the level where they actually arise — that of political effectiveness and not of scholarship. Why question the facile but fragile success gained by fictitious historical views if it is not because such success conceals errors, political traps, gaps, of which scientific 'inaccuracy' is only the outward sign?

Because they underestimated the class antagonisms of old Saxon England, the utopian Levellers were unprepared to cope with the exploiting classes of the seventeenth century. Because they uncritically accepted an idealized image of the Roman Republic, the democratic forces of the French Revolution were ill-prepared to deal with a rising bourgeoisie whose only aim was to deflect to its own ends the revolutionary movement against the feudal monarchy. Because they accept an idyllic concept of Occitania before its conquest by northern France, the Occitan militants are unable to win the movement over from the privileged classes, who are the more interested in changing their relations with Paris than with the local working class. And the Occitan Left, which is aware of these traps and ambiguities, demands that the Count of Toulouse, Raimond VII, 'be buried once and for all' rather than being preserved as

a symbol. It denounces not only the centralist myth of an eternal, un-
changeable France, but also the

> mythology, so pleasant to regional ears, of an Occitanian golden age —
> a mythology as false and dangerous as the earlier one, because equally
> nationalistic; it originated with the songs of the Albigensian crusade
> and reappeared with Mistral and Company.
>   The myth of the thirteenth century in Occitania plays a dual role.
> It consoles the people who have never become reconciled to the defeat
> of the Occitanian nobility by the Paris king at Muret in 1213; unable
> to create a real Occitania in their own day and age, they retreat into
> an opium-dream. But it also projects the picture of a bourgeois demo-
> cratic society of tolerance, equality and cultural refinement: the
> ideology of the provincial middle classes with no real impact of
> history. . . . These dreams must be ended, for they only obscure the
> meaning of the Occitan struggle which is taking place in the present
> and not in the past.*

Here as elsewhere the stakes are political. Scientific accuracy is not
an abstract intellectual demand but the precondition of a coherent political analysis:

'Whoever invents false revolutionary legends for the people, amuses
them with lyrical tales, is no less guilty than a geographer who draws up
misleading maps for navigators.'**

For the peoples engaged in the fight for national and social liberation,
the past is a political issue, a theme of struggle. It is also an occasion to
proclaim the necessity of a new departure in the direction of a qualitatively different world. But that cannot be done without abandoning the
conventional historical framework and its chronology as well. The
qualitative thereby asserts its primacy over the quantitative, discontinuity
over continuity. There is a feeling that we must start at 'zero', and many
a revolutionary movement has proclaimed its 'Year 01' (0 + 1) to mark
its break with the established social system through a *break with the
established calendar*. This is something the people understand — immediately! The French Republic of 1792, the Chinese Republic of 1912, both
inaugurated new calendars as a symbol of the advent of a new age and
the downfall of the secular monarchies that had taken possession of the
very structure of time itself. In China following the liberation in 1949,
the calendar — for various practical reasons — was not changed, but the
accent was placed on the coming of a new era (*shidai*, an almost cosmic
term), and on the fact that, from that moment onward, 'times had
changed', as the peasants say.

* *Forabunda* (Bulletin Occitan de Paris), 3.
** Lissagaray, *Histoire de la Commune*.

4 Was Marx an 'historian'?

Marxism as a continuous creation on the basis of social practice – not a discourse on 'world history' – the false schematism of the 'five stages' – Marx proceeds directly from the present: he is not a 'Marxist historian' – reasoning historically about the present in order to change it

The revolutionary theory elaborated by Marx and Engels, developed in action by Rosa Luxemburg and Lenin, by Gramsci and Mao Ze-dong, is an *historically based* theory. It was by analyzing *both* the society of their time and the earlier stages in the history of human societies that the theoreticians of Marxism defined the stakes, the directions, the aims of the struggle against the bourgeois order and capitalist exploitation, with a view to building a socialist society (or socialist societies). The basic concepts of historical materialism apply to the totality of societies known to history, including the one in which we live.

These basic concepts are a continuous creation. They are deepened and expanded at each important stage of the struggle for socialism. Lenin emphasized the concrete international contradictions of capitalism, the uneven impact of its extension around the globe, the conflict between imperialism and the oppressed countries. Under the impetus of the workers' struggle that took place in the aftermath of the First World War, Gramsci stressed the complexity of the superstructure. The 'civil society' (family, culture, social relations, etc.) is more fragile, he pointed out, than the 'political' society and can become an autonomous, if not the principal, field of revolutionary activity. Intellectuals can break away from the ruling class and its ideology to become 'organically' linked to the oppressed classes and the revolution. Chinese communism, whose rise dominated the entire socialist movement of the twentieth century, also made some extremely significant creative contributions to Marxism, such as: the concept of 'putting politics in command', which brings out the role of collective consciousness as opposed to economic determinism; the universality of contradiction; the political capacities of the peasantry; the failure of the state and party apparatus in some socialist countries to prevent the emergence of a privileged neo-bourgeoisie; the reversibility

or revocability of the socialist achievements so long as a capitalist environment exists outside the country and relations of 'bourgeois law' prevail
within it.

The basic Marxist concepts − mode of production, class struggle, the
decisive role of the economic factor in the last analysis, the universality
of contradiction − are neither 'old-fashioned' nor 'outdated' as successive
generations of intellectuals in France repeated after being disillusioned
by the ebb of the 1917−19 upsurge, or of the Popular Front, or of the
Liberation in 1945, or of May '68. It is still impossible to analyze properly
the history of the Chinese Revolution, for example, or that of the Fifth
Republic in France, without reference to the dominant mode of production in each country, or to the relationship between the forces of production, the relations of production and the superstructure, or to the role
of economic processes, to the class struggle, to primary and secondary
contradictions. But recognizing all that is *only the beginning*. The task that
remains is to analyze and explain events and developments in terms of
concrete conditions.

For while Marxist theory is based on history, it is not a 'theory of
history' or a new version of the 'discourse on world history' for which
so many historians nourish a kind of nostalgia. In other words, its main
function is not, and never has been, to provide a general, rigid, ready-
made explanation of the history of human societies as they developed
chronologically and specifically. This applies, first of all, to the successive
modes of production. Marxist theory does not, as a matter of principle,
reduce world history to an inexorable succession of dominant modes of
production as in the Stalinist theory of the 'five stages'. These modes of
production characterize certain *types* of society − slavery, feudalism,
capitalism − which are only rarely encountered in their 'pure' forms.
There are numerous intermediary or marginal situations. Most countries
in the European Middle Ages represented only an imperfect form of
feudalism and most of the countries of the Third World today are only
partially capitalist systems. The various modes of production, moreover,
are staggered throughout space and time, with a whole series of gaps that
are not directly explained in Marxist theory, since it does not operate
at that level. These gaps must be analyzed in Marxist terms, but at the
level of concrete historical experience.

These modes of production do not follow one another in a linear
sequence, with every people inevitably passing through them all. Such
a unilinear conception long prevented any real discussion of the 'Asiatic'
mode of production that was glimpsed by Marx but ignored by Soviet
Marxists since Stalin. In China, it is referred to only indirectly in connection with the 'specific features' of Chinese feudalism and slavery, such
as the existence of an important state bureaucracy whose power was based

on its function, and the absence of private ownership of land during the 'slavery' period. The 'Asiatic' Mode of Production (A.M.P.), which Marx defined as a combined form of state power based on an economic 'high command' and a series of practically self-sufficient village communities, helps us analyze the original characteristics of many pre-capitalist societies that do not fit the Marxist description of slavery or feudalism, since *production* is carried out neither through private slavery nor personal serfdom.

Nor does Marxism provide a ready-made formula for the history of each people. Such distinct histories consist of a whole series of concrete mechanisms, lags, obstacles, regional differences, retreats, interruptions, resurgences, survivals, that are not directly dealt with in the body of Marxist principles. The analysis of all such concrete mechanisms must be carried out within the general framework of Marxist theory, however — and that is by no means easy.

The degradation of Marxism to the level of economic fatalism is particularly dangerous. In this view, the succession of modes of production is fated to occur regardless of what happens. 'The great wheel of history turns' and socialism is bound to come about inevitably as a result of the 'objective' contradictions between the forces and the relations of production. In that case, we have only to await the fulfilment of the 'objective conditions'. And socialism, once established, will in this view be unassailable. But the Chinese, in their critique of Soviet revisionism, have put forward the idea that retreats and relapses are always possible. This again is a completely new contribution. Marx, as a child of the nineteenth century and an heir of the Enlightenment, was certainly imbued with a confidence and optimism about human progress that the crises of the twentieth century have not confirmed. History advances by spirals, say the Chinese. The metaphor can be taken for what it is worth, but it does have the merit of stressing the complex play of advances and retreats that mark the development of societies.

Marxism, a theory of revolutionary struggle and not intended for purely intellectual analysis, arose from the necessities of social practice. It studies past centuries only to return better armed to the struggles of the present. In the following passage, Engels clearly expressed the primacy of practice and the demands of the present:

The new facts [*i.e.,* the 1831 revolt of the workers in Lyons and the British Chartist movement] made imperative a new examination of all past history. Then it was seen that *all* past history was the history of class struggles; that these warring classes of society are always the products of the modes of production and exchange — in a word, of the *economic* conditions of their time; that the economic structure of society always furnishes the real basis, starting from which we can work out the ultimate explanation of the whole super-structure of juridical and political institutions as well as of the religious, philosophical and other ideas of a given historical period. . . . Now idealism was driven from its last refuge, the philosophy of history; now a materialistic treatment of history was propounded, and a method found of explaining man's 'knowing' by his 'being', instead of, as heretofore, his 'being' by his 'knowing'.

From that time forward, socialism was no longer an accidental discovery of this or that ingenious brain, but the necessary outcome of the struggle between two historically developed classes – the proletariat and the bourgeoisie. Its task was no longer to manufacture a system of society as perfect as possible, but to examine the historico-economic succession of events from which those classes and their antagonism had of necessity sprung, and to discover in the economic conditions thus created the means of ending the conflict.*

Marxism, then, represents not only a reversal of the conventional philosophical approach ('Turn the old idealism right side up, stand it on its feet'), as we have all learned to repeat by rote, but also a reversal of the conventional historical approach – for Marxism, it is the past that is governed by the present and not the other way around. And this aspect of the problem is so upsetting to our normal way of thinking that it is usually avoided – by 'Marxist historians' as much as by anyone else.

Henri Lefevre, in his work *La Fin de l'histoire*, stressed this reversal of outlook:

Marx clearly indicated the historian's approach. *He begins with the present* – practical experience, concepts in the process of being developed – and cannot do otherwise. His approach is a recurrent one. He proceeds from the present to the past. After which, he returns to present reality, now analyzed and grasped, rather than trying to analyze a confused whole. This methodological principle – or precept – is valid generally. The adult enables us to understand the child and the man the monkey – not the other way around. Neither the child nor the monkey can be isolated from the global future of which they are but moments of history – natural, social or psychological. There remains enough of the child in the adult, moreover, and enough of the monkey in the man so that the investigation can come back to the present whose distinctive features and concrete development will be better understood.

In the same way, according to Marx, bourgeois society throws light retrospectively on feudal society: the capitalist economy throws light on the economy of the Middle Ages and Antiquity. Ground rent and its role under capitalism must be studied to understand the phenomenon of income from the land in other societies – tribute, the tithe, the *corvée*, various forms of rent. 'Bourgeois society is the most highly developed and diversified form of social organization in history. The categories that express relationships within this society and explain its structure also

* F. Engels, *Anti-Duhring.*

enable us to grasp the structure and relations of production in societies of the past.'*

In their struggle against capitalism, Marx and the workers for whom he was the spokesman tried to grasp it in its historical perspective as a temporary phenomenon; they studied its origins in order to define and predict the circumstances of its downfall. They intended to show that capitalism was only the passing form of a more general category, the mode of production, which had assumed other forms in the past and would therefore assume still others in the future. To lay bare the mechanism of capitalist exploitation as it operated before their eyes, Marx and Engels had to show where it came from in the hope of showing that it could be brought to an end, just as other historical modes of production had come to an end. They had to define the inner nature of these other modes of production and determine their basic laws. Marx analyzes older societies — classical Asia, Greece and Rome, the Middle Ages — so as to give more general substance to the 'mode of production' category. *His analysis goes no further than that.*

Marx, then, was not a 'Marxist historian' in the sense in which the expression is used in the 'left-wing' academic circles of Paris, Moscow or Tokyo where the Party apparatus and the institutional hierarchy of the university comfortably merge or cooperate. Marx never looked upon the study of the past as an intellectual activity for its own sake, an autonomous field of knowledge. To take an example cited by the French Marxist historian P. Vilar, he never tried to write even a brief outline of the history of Spain, which he knew intimately. He was more interested in *analyzing historically* — that is, politically — *the Spain of his time.*

It is therefore useless and ridiculous to entertain, as some do, the ambition of becoming 'the Marx of feudalism'. For such an attitude loses sight of the underlying principle of Marxism: the primacy of social practice. For Marx, the aim was not simply to understand the world, *but to change it.* This introduces an essential, qualitative difference between our study of capitalist society and our study of the societies of the past. It was not because of 'lack of time', as some suggest with a sigh of regret, that Marx never produced a coherent, systematic analysis of the ancient 'Asiatic' societies, of ancient Greece and Rome, or the feudal Middle Ages, but confined himself to remarks scattered here and there throughout his work. His 'historical culture' was broad enough, surely, for such a task! But his choice was political: a detailed and systematic knowledge of the past was not an end-in-itself for him. Marx may not have been a 'Marxist historian' but he was certainly a revolutionary intellectual. His intellectual activity had no other object than to stimulate the people's

* K. Marx, *Grundrisse.*

struggles, to support them to the extent of his ability and — together with those involved in such struggles — to clarify their goals and perspectives.

It would be forgetting the basic aim of Marxism to plunge with scholarly relish into the minute study — as if these were isolated fields of knowledge — of the French Revolution, for example, of Greek civilization, of modern Spain, or even of peasant revolts or the labour movement, using the theoretical tools of Marxism. For to do so would be *turning those tools from their true function*.

While the 'Marxist historian' operates in a sphere removed from social practice, there is still a place — and a need — for a study of the past, both recent and long ago, which is explicitly linked to current mass struggles in both its questions and its responses, and which makes full use of the theoretical insights of Marxism. Not the usual academic historical rhetoric couched in Marxist phraseology, but an *active* relationship to the past, based on Marxism. What kind of history does the Revolution need?

5 Reversing the past ↔ present relationship

Winding the reel backwards — historical work as field work — can the present help us 'understand the past' — the present sharpens the profile of the past — rewriting is justified — Dario Fo as an 'operational historian' of the Middle Ages — Amin Dada as a critical historian

The definition of history as an active relationship to the past implies the reversal of the conventional past-present relationship. 'Man resembles his time more than he does his father.' Marc Bloch, who was fond of quoting this Arab proverb, was sharply critical of what he called 'the adulation of origins'. We have to 'wind the reel backwards', he would say — in other words, start with the known in order to grasp the threads leading backward in time. In *Apologie pour l'histoire,* he insists on the indispensable value of practical daily experience, on what he calls 'constant contact with the here and now':

> How often had I read — and told — stories of wars and battles. Did I really know, in the full sense of the word, know *from within,* what it means for an army to be surrounded, for a people to be defeated, before I myself experienced the deep *nausea* of such a situation? . . . In fact, whether consciously or not, it is always, in the last analysis, from daily experience that we take the elements we need to reconstitute the past. . . . The scholar who has no taste for watching people, things, events round him might be a useful antiquarian but he would hardly be justified in describing himself as an historian.

We have all, at one time or another, experienced the stimulating effect of the present in sharpening our appreciation of the past. My visit to Alma-Ata in 1967 was not merely a descent into historical emptiness. Although that city is known throughout the world as the place of Trotsky's banishment before his exile, when I mentioned its famous guest, I could rouse no reaction whatever among the people with whom I spoke — a case of deliberate occultation for the older people, of complete ignorance for the younger generation. But Alma-Ata is something else again. It is a huge city located at the foot of the magnificent Altai mountains and its very location produces a sharp, almost physical, sense of the political isolation suffered by the outlawed leader in 1930. At the same time, in near-by China on the other side of the mountains, there was occurring the first concrete collective experience of a communist revolution that had broken with the bureaucratic dogmatism of the Comintern, thanks to the Mao-inspired 'mass line' and the mobilization of the peasantry. Thus on each side of the Altai mountains around the year 1930, two distinct types of challenge to Stalinism, two lines of opposition that were and are irreconcilable, were taking shape: a minority courageously clinging to its intellectual opposition, and the collective struggle to wage a people's revolution, thereby defying the Comintern *in practice* (Mao refused, for example, to attack the cities in 1931 in obedience to Moscow). On the spot, all this was felt with an almost obsessive acuteness.

Similarly, my visit in 1969 to the *ghost-farming* landscape just north of Boston brought home to me in the same poignant way the whole historical problem of regression. Today, that area near Tilton is covered by huge forests with no other inhabitants than a scattering of Harvard University people who spend their week-ends there. The prosperous villages that had flourished ever since pre-Revolutionary times had to be abandoned in the face of the massive competition from the cereal-producing areas of the Middle West towards the end of the nineteenth century. The forests earlier cleared by the Puritans had gradually re-conquered the area, leaving here and there the forgotten sign of a farm life that had once been as active as the Cornish or Norman countryside — an empty chimney, a small stone wall, the remains of an enclosure, an untended apple-tree that had returned to its natural state. It is strange that historians have been so contemptuous of the 'field work' that is fashionable among sociologists, anthropologists, linguists — so much so that it often represents the essential, decisive step in a 'splendid career' ('Oh yes! His field-trip to New Guinea!'). Yet Michelet wrote at length of what he derived from his travels around France and Bloch of his discussions with peasants or town-hall clerks.

Examples abound of the extent to which our knowledge of the past is subordinated to the demands of the world in which we live, whether at the level of 'scientific' works or of books for the general public. French scholarly works on the Crusades or the Latin states of Syria have had two distinct periods of popularity, as any graduate student who has dipped into the bibliography knows — one under Napoleon III who sent an Army to Lebanon, and another around 1920–40 at the time of the French 'mandate' over the region. Consciously or not, interest in the subject was politically motivated — historians, archaeologists, palaeographers, numismatists, outdid each other in an effort to confer 'historical legitimacy' upon this venture of French imperialism. The fact that the present shapes our approach to the past can take the more ridiculous form of fashionableness as in the case of a French university textbook on the Middle Ages that added to a new post-'68 edition a section on 'marginalism' in order to be up-to-date. The busy author simply included the famous description of the Court of Miracles from Victor Hugo's *Notre Dame de Paris,* without realizing that these pages are based on seventeenth-century material.

The connection with present-day concerns is often more explicit. We have already mentioned the Gauls and the American cowboys, for example (p. 11). The recent appearance of a book on *La Femme Celte* (The Celtic Woman) can be interpreted in no other way than as a reflection of the current upsurge of the women's movement. Our stock of written documents about the Celts has not changed since Roman times and will probably not do so in the future, although archaeological excavations may deepen our knowledge. Yet it is today and not in the seventeenth century – when the ancient Roman historians were far better known than they are now – that such a book was written.

These examples emphasize the vital and stimulating role of the present. But the 'perpetual contact with today', as Marc Bloch expressed it, does not in itself lead to a genuine reversal of the conventional past-present relation. The title of the chapter of Bloch's work from which the above-quoted words are taken is, in fact, 'Understanding the Past through the Present'. Understanding the past still remains, then, the historian's main aim. The recourse to the present is seen as merely one of the 'tricks of the trade', a pedagogical or heuristic device, a skilful means of discovering some good leads and making history 'interesting'. At best, it is an aspect of professional conscience. 'If I can talk to them first about the struggles of the Black ghettos of the United States,' said a knowledgeable woman historian of my acquaintance, 'I will succeed in getting my students interested in the history of nineteenth-century Africa, *which is where I want to take them.*' But we must go one step further, break completely with the conventional attitude and proclaim *as a matter of principle* the primacy of the present over the past. And that is something historians do not like.

So it is not enough to say with Daniel Guérin – and Marc Bloch before him – that the present contributes to an *understanding* of the past, although such an approach is useful and all too rare among historians:

> The class struggles of the present time, the revolutions of today, throw new light on the class struggles and revolutions of the past.
>   Guizot, conservative that he was, had caught a glimpse of that. In the preface to his *Histoire de la Révolution d'Angleterre*, he draws on the experience of the French Revolution to show that the English

Revolution 'would never have been so well understood if the French Revolution had not occurred'. He adds that 'without the French Revolution and the light it spread on the struggle between the Stuarts and the English people, nineteenth-century works on the English Revolution would have none of the new qualities that distinguish them.'

We shall simply adopt Guizot's reasoning and apply it to the present. Just as the French Revolution enabled us to understand the English Revolution, so the French Revolution takes on new meaning as a result of the 'new light' the revolutions of the twentieth century shed on the class struggle — then still in its embryonic stage — between the bourgeoisie and the masses of people in 1793. Today, we have the 'advantage' over our predecessors, the historians of the French Revolution, of being in a position to 'observe and judge' it from the vantage point of experiences like the Russian Revolutions of 1905 and 1917, the German Revolution of 1918, the Italian crisis of 1920, the Spanish Revolution of 1936–39 — not forgetting the latest experience, one we not only studied but *lived through*: the intense social upheaval of June 1936 in France.

Take the example of communal or 'soviet' democracy. The Paris Commune foreshadowed the Russian Soviets and the Bolsheviks carefully studied the French experiences of 1793 and 1871 to gain a better understanding of the one that was taking place before their eyes. But at the same time, the experience of the Soviets in 1905, and even more in 1917, enables us now to recognize in the Commune of 1793 the embryo of the soviet concealed within the thick shell (purposely exaggerated by the historians) of Parliamentary democracy.*

The point is that historical thinking operates *regressively — in a direction opposite to the flow of time —* and this is its basic reason for being. The survivors of the huge inter-imperialist slaughter of 1914–18 had just lived through a war of immense scope and terrifying intensity: they instinctively called it the Great War. When the war of 1937–39–'41–'45 (its starting point varied from one continent to the other) spread over the entire world, its global character was its most distinctive aspect. As a result, people became aware retrospectively of the global nature of the 'First' World War. From that time on, the First World War has been described with reference to the Second. The expression, 'The Great War' is rarely heard today.

When they called for a boycott of the 8 March celebration in 1975 — the UN's International Woman's Year — the militant French feminists deliberately returned to the past, not to commemorate certain selected dates but to restore their links with history in order to live more intensely in the present:

1972: The UN decrees an 'International WOMAN's Year'.
1974: Giscard d'Estaing's government creates a Secretary of State for Women's Condition.

*D. Guérin, *La Lutte des classes sous la Première République*.

1975: A campaign is launched to integrate women into the Establishment, co-opt our struggles, censor our history.

March 8, 1857: One of the first women's strikes in the United States pits textile workers against the New York police who charge them and open fire.

March 8, 1910: The International Congress of Socialist Women, at the suggestion of Clara Zetkin, calls for an International Day of Action.

March 8, 1917 (February 23, by the Russian Calendar): The Russian Revolution begins with a women's demonstration.

March 8, 1943: The women of Italy organize a demonstration against male fascism.

On March 8, 1975, we shall revive our links with this tradition of women's struggles. Not simply to commemorate it, but to *proclaim* that our history did not begin with a UN decree or a speech by Françoise Giroud.

On March 8, 1975, we shall refuse to let ourselves be confined to a gimmicky 'Woman's Year', an official program, a date. It is a moment of our daily struggle, of our solidarity with the struggle of the women in every country.*

The primacy of the present over the past is based on the fact that it is the present alone that forces us to change the world. We return once again to Marx's original thought – that we understand the child through the adult and the monkey through the man, since it is the adult and the man who are *masters of their future.* The end of historical knowledge is practical action, struggle. In China, they say *Gu wei jin yong*: 'Put the past at the service of the present.' The study of the dissident intellectuals of the feudal period, the legists who fiercely opposed the Confucian powers-that-be, reinforced the recent anti-Confucius campaign and contributed to current efforts to do away with the ancient attitudes of servility imposed by Confucian rules and still amazingly alive after thirty years of socialism: domination by the males, by knowledge, by the bureaucrats, by the 'talented people', by the past. In China, the peasant wars that were constantly waged against the Hans, the Tangs, the Songs, the Mings, gave the peasants confidence in their political ability and so prepared them for the revolution as well as for the subsequent period of socialist construction and the fight against the development of a neo-bourgeoisie. For the American sinologists and their friends, this is a pure case of 'rewriting', the unforgivable sin of the 'scientific' historian. But this new viewpoint is new only in the sense that it brings out facts previously concealed by conventional historians or regarded as of secondary importance, glossed over in the academic textbooks. This new writing – if it avoids the real dangers of distortion and over-simplification – contributes both to a better understanding of the past

---

*From a leaflet distributed by French feminist groups in March 1975.

and to a better orientation of the political movement today. Historical accuracy and political intransigence are complementary.

What matters is the *operational* character of the relationship to the past, its relevance to the demands of the present, not its chronological distance. The Middle Ages, at least in France, are generally regarded as the stronghold of historical conservatism. Country squires and honorary canons conduct research about the Middle Ages on a volunteer basis. Medieval Christianity is idealized by the Right. And 'Son et Lumiere' shows are organized in the castles and cathedrals every summer for the benefit of tourists. On the other hand, there are aspects of the Middle Ages that speak directly to us and are linked to our present concerns and struggles, which they can clarify and strengthen.

This is the attitude of the English Romantics. For them, the Middle Ages was a time of struggle and a 'survival instrument' against capitalism:

> Tradition is not a remnant but an instrument of survival; not folklore but a pole of opposition to organized and intensified destitution. Its role is to reveal what the institutions have repressed.
> The romantics dug up the Celtic world, the Middle Ages, to find in the past the images required to develop attitudes of anti-commercial and anti-industrial nostalgia. Just as primitive democracy is the mythical repressed element of the state systems, the feudal values — for example, honour, respect for women — constitute the repressed element, however imaginary, of relations based on money and profit. The historical memory is not neutral. Inspired by nostalgia and anger, romantic historiography strives, like individual memory, to counteract traumatic recollections by drawing from the myth of imaginary happiness the certainty that another happiness is possible.*

In Italy, the leftist actor and director, Dario Fo, tried in the 1970s to create a militant political theatre with roots in the past. This approach led him also to the Middle Ages. He plunged into a study of the popular urban theatre of medieval Lombardy, using highly specialized palaeo-graphic techniques, since these works are virtually unavailable in a modern version. His approach was a militant one. By reviving the basic irreverence of this rich repertoire of plays and performing them before popular audiences, Dario Fo was affirming, without sermonizing, the political and cultural capacity of the people, in the past and therefore in the present. He was helping them in their struggle against the capitalist system. Dario Fo's group (Collectivo Teatrale *La Commune*) travelled throughout Italy with these ancient plays, most of which were previously unknown even to the most erudite scholars.

There are many other contributions that the Middle Ages can make to an understanding of the problems of our time. For example, the workers' struggles of today are often imbued with the narrow craft

* Paul Rosenberg, *Le Romanticisme Anglais.*

spirit that was pervasive during the Middle Ages. And even under the capitalist system of a 'free labour market', extra-economic compulsion — the use of violence and physical or ideological force — plays an important role in social life. The immigrant workers know this better than anyone else — the system they work under is not really one of pure 'wage-labour', since the meagre wages they receive are accompanied by innumerable forms of violence and intimidation. The extra-economic compulsion that seeps insidiously into capitalist relationships was at the very heart of the feudal mode of production. The Middle Ages is not so far removed from our concerns, after all. Similarly, medieval architecture is more than a curiosity for vacationers and archaeologists — it is an ideological symbol endowed with a political function. Its constructions are an essential characteristic of the power structure a powerful instrument of social segregation and political control. This relationship between the established order and its architecture, particularly evident during the Middle Ages, is no less real today, although it takes a different form. We must decode the political function of the constructions in which we are enclosed — towers, highways, suburban residential areas and supermarkets, inactive 'green' areas, etc.

In these examples of the relevance of medieval history, what counts is the *explicit* relationship between our problems, our struggles, and the existing historical knowledge of various aspects of the Middle Ages. The past→present relationship is based on silence, occultation, isolation, the unspoken; the reverse relationship — present→past — must be explicit and openly proclaimed, thus politicized. Reversing the relation between past and present often means inverting accepted symbols, changing the conventional meaning of certain facts. From earliest childhood, we in France are given a positive image of Duguesclin as a hero of the fight against the English in the Middle Ages; for the Breton militants, the Breton consciousness, he was a traitor to Brittany, a 'collaborator' of the kings of France.

One more example — and a disturbing one. Whatever can be said of Amin Dada, he leaves nobody indifferent. His every gesture tells. He is a pure product of British imperialism, and the criticism of his 'brutal' methods of rule should first be directed to the 'skilful' decolonization techniques of which the British are so proud. For the first concern of the British, when they finally recognized the necessity of abandoning their Empire, was to make sure, before leaving the colonies, that no popular revolution would be possible there; to this end, they placed in power new 'élites', usually military men trained in the British colonial army. But Amin Dada, an ex-sergeant of the British Army, happens to be a past master in a style of derision that is loaded with political and historical significance.

When he arrived at the Conference of African States in 1975 on a sedan chair carried by four British businessmen from Uganda, his behaviour struck home more quickly and deeply than dozens of pamphlets denouncing the hypocrisy of colonialism and the White Man's Burden. 'Of course, I *could* walk,' he remarked to the journalists, 'but what about the days when you were carried by Blacks?'

'To enable man to understand the society of the past and to increase his mastery over the society of the present': this was the formula used by E. H. Carr to describe history's dual function. He was right – but it is the second part of the statement that alone gives meaning to the first.

6 The false assumptions of historical rhetoric

*The cult of the historical fact, primary sources and secondary works –
diachrony and synchrony, periodization, quantification: is all that indispensable to historical accuracy? – is any historian certain to be read by
future generations? – its technicism, intellectualism and productivism
make historical rhetoric part of the prevailing ideology*

Among 'professionals', certain things are taken for granted. In any case,
the experienced professor is amazed when the neophyte researcher refuses to accept his version of the truth. This type of implicit indoctrination is extremely effective and helps to strengthen and perpetuate the
historian's profession. But these false assumptions must not be accepted
at face value.

Consider, for example, the *historical fact* which is supposedly true or
false once and for all; historians try to establish its absolute objectivity,
its pure reality. This nineteenth-century positivism is deeply rooted in
the minds of historians. It fails to take into account either the impact of
human observation on all phenomena, or their internal contradictions. In
the Anglo-Saxon world, even more openly than in France, this pragmatic
positivism finds expression in the basic distinction that is made, from
elementary school onwards, between *facts* and *values*. The former supposedly exist independently – in the absolute – while the latter are an
expression of each individual's subjective attitude (how liberal we are!).
But it is out of the question to analyze the relationship between the
two.

Rejecting this positivism does not mean taking refuge in a cynical relativism ('Everyone is entitled to his own version of historical truth!').
Historical facts can be known scientifically, but this implies an understanding of their specific characteristics. On the one hand, such facts are
contradictory, as is the course of history in general. They are perceived
differently – because they are differently distorted – in different times
and places, among different social classes and ideological currents. At
the same time, they cannot be directly experienced, since they belong
to the past – they can be known only by progressive approximations to a

reality that is never completely attained. The demand for scientific accuracy, indispensable as a defence against falsification and myths, tends to 'free' the facts from distortion and obscurity; the aim is to increase the precision of our knowledge, making it richer and more genuine. And this can be achieved, not through the historian's political 'neutrality' or 'objectivity', but only through involvement in the political struggle. There is need for a denunciation of the political biases leading to false interpretations and deliberate gaps — they are linked to practices of alienation and oppression in the interests of the power structure and the ruling classes. The objectivity and realism of our knowledge can be constantly perfected as current economic problems enable us to study the past with increasing sharpness and accuracy.

> The historian's impartiality is only a myth serving to reinforce conventional attitudes. It is a myth that should have been destroyed by the works about the First World War. History is always 'a child of its time', rooted in a social class, a country, a political environment. But the only kind of frank partiality that is compatible today with the greatest concern for the truth is that of the working-class historian. For the working class alone has everything to gain, regardless of the circumstances, from a knowledge of the truth. It has nothing to hide — in the historical record, at least. The role of historical lies has always been — and still is — to deceive the working class. It refutes them to win, and wins by refuting them.*

Sinologists comfortably settled in the tranquillity of their studies would never have been in a position to free Chinese history from the Mandarin outlook — with its emphasis on the dynastic cycles, the Heavenly Mandate, etc. — and stress the role of the masses, especially of peasant rebellions, in the development of imperial China. Dozens of scholarly monographs have been published concerning Chinese urban architecture — in particular, the walls surrounding the cities. And yet the architects, with their traditional indifference to political issues, never explained the real function of those walls. Located in many cases thousands of kilometres from the borders, they could not have been built to protect the cities from invasions; at the same time, the wars between feudal lords that ravaged Western Europe during the Middle Ages were unknown in China for over two thousand years. The city walls have a *class* function — to defend the imperial power structure and its bureaucracy, a highly developed institution in this 'Asiatic' society, from outbursts of peasant wrath. But only those who are involved in the struggles of the peasants, as are the historians of People's China, can understand and stress the weight of the peasantry in the dynastic history of China. Those who are so involved

* Victor Serge, *L'An 1 de la révolution*, foreword.

have not merely substituted one subjective attitude for another; they have achieved a basic new outlook.

Primary sources and *secondary works:* the first thing every historian does is examine the bibliography of a colleague or a beginner whose work he intends to 'judge' or evaluate. A good bibliography is expected to make a clear-cut distinction between 'primary sources' and the works of other historians, 'secondary sources'. Thus historians claim a special status for their writings about the past. The work of their 'colleagues', however ancient, is carefully distinguished from other materials such as laws, public acts, administrative documents, private correspondence, public speeches, etc. But this conventional separation is based on a false assumption. For every type of material — regardless of its nature or date, whether contemporaneous with the facts or posterior to them — only partially reflects historical reality. Rather, the materials *refract* reality, in terms of the concerns, the individual or collective interests, of those who collect and use them. The historian is no more neutral than the legislator, the scribe, the archivist, the writer of memoirs, the letter-writer.

How should we classify, for example, the *Report on the Peasant Movement of Hunan*, written in 1927 by Mao Ze-dong, a classic of the literature on the Chinese peasantry? And how should we classify Lenin's *Imperialism: The Highest Stage of Capitalism*? Is it a primary source or a secondary work? The answer would be as meaningless as the question. The more a work is linked — as are those of Mao or Lenin — to political concerns, the more they elude the technical categories of the professional historian and the more clearly they demonstrate the falseness of his approach.

Diachrony-synchrony: always eager to outfit Clio, the Muse of History, with new clothes designed in patchwork fashion, historians have borrowed these two categories from the formalistic linguistics initiated in Western Europe by Leopold Saussure. In this view, every historical fact, like every linguistic fact, can be analyzed both in a vertical series along the time-dimension (the diachrony), and in a horizontal series with reference to the social complex to which it belongs (the synchrony). This method of analysis is based on another false assumption — that the totality of the past is uniformly worth of attention and study. The fanatics of the synchrony-diachrony scheme would crucify man by fixating him at the intersection of these two immutable dimensions. They would pitilessly square off the historical field.

But there is room today for a different kind of relationship to the past. If we must have diagrams, we might imagine — instead of the synchrony-diachrony pattern of squares to which the observer is *external* — a kind of spiral with the observer at its centre, *inside* the historical field. This spiral moves away from the observer as it recedes in time, but he establishes a *direct* relationship with each point in the past, *selectively*,

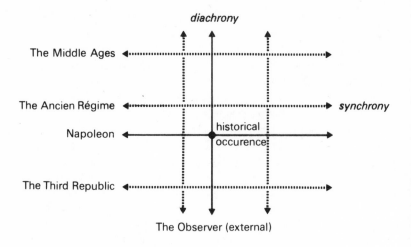

diachrony

The Middle Ages

The Ancien Régime — synchrony

Napoleon — historical occurence

The Third Republic

The Observer (external)

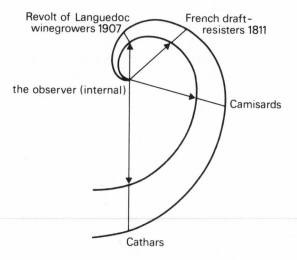

Revolt of Languedoc winegrowers 1907

French draft-resisters 1811

the observer (internal)

Camisards

Cathars

in terms of contemporary concerns. *The relationship between our own time and each age of the past is of more significance than the relationship of each past age to the rest of historical time.* Let the dead bury the dead!

Periodization: this can be considered as an extension, a refinement, of diachrony. Not only does the historian give special attention to the succession of facts in time, their 'genealogy', but his main task is to organize and establish a rhythm for this time-flux, to identify the pivotal moments, the more or less static phases and the sudden accelerations — the 'periods', in a word. This is an expression of the old nostalgia for a 'discourse on world history', a favourite practice of the official dynastic chroniclers of all countries, as well as of the philosophers of the rising bourgeoisie, such as Voltaire, Volney, Gibbon. It took on new life with academic Marxism, particularly in the Soviet Union. The chronological flux is presented there as a massive, homogeneous process external to the student of it — and the ability to divide it up with a show of competence is considered proof of mastery over the principles of historical materialism. At Moscow University, the annual study programme was laid out in such a way that the reign of Kangxi, the greatest Manchu Emperor, was split in 1688, as if the English Revolution of that date was a dividing-line for China, i.e., as if the political rise of the bourgeoisie had taken place in China at the same time as in the West.

The periodizing mania is further accentuated by pedagogical practice; since history's only professed aim is to provide a neutral record of the succession of events in time, independently of the human will, reference-points and historical landmarks are indispensable. And so the professionals divide and subdivide the military history of the First World War, the history of the negotiations over the Vienna Treaty or of the National Assemblies during the French Revolution — a game as endless as it is meaningless.

Once again, a mere study technique, justifiable in certain cases only, has been converted into a basic assumption. An accurate determination of the phases of the May '68 movement, for example, is needed because the study of the event has a definite political function: it enables us to understand better how a major crisis breaks out and develops in a country like contemporary France. It might also be useful to gain a better grasp of how events much further in the past could be periodized, but only if it were done in terms that are meaningful to us, since we do need to know how *political* situations can be suddenly reversed and how mutations occur — in the past and therefore in the present.

Quantification: It has been said that the only scientific history is quantitative history. But a study technique cannot be regarded as more important than the basic aim of the study itself. The quantifiers persistently ignore the degree of uncertainty and even subjectivity in the figures they feed into their insatiable computers. Those figures are worth no more than the intentions, the ignorance, the assumptions of the person who compiles them — in other words, his ideology. Take the statistics for the prison population in contemporary France. They are established by the officials of the Ministry of Justice for whom the social function of imprisonment is to guarantee the strict enforcement of the law. So the inmates are classified as first offenders and recidivists, or according to the type of court that condemned them and the nature of their offense. But all these carefully kept statistics tell us nothing about the real social significance of 'crime'. How many inmates, for example, are in prison because of the greed inspired by the capitalist law of profit? And how many are there simply because of hard times and destitution? How many have acted from resentment, confusion or psychological unbalance? Here the quantifiers' computers can tell us nothing. Only through intellectual elaboration, through *qualitative* analysis of representative cases, can we hope to establish a typology — one that would never be quantifiable. Yet such a qualitative analysis of the motivations of crime is infinitely more operational and teaches us far more than the quantitative approach.

The meticulous techniques of historical demography, transposed on the political space of colonial Africa, are also of only limited value. Birth certificates, cattle head-counts, even vaccination records — all are systematically faked by the village chiefs. They know very well that such quantitative information is not intended for the historian's computers but for the tax collector.

A similar example is the sterile investigation carried out by John Lossing Buck, an American missionary in Nanking. Around 1930, he described the Chinese rural society with a plethora of figures and tables. His figures were arranged in accordance with the 'variables' borrowed from the American capitalist agriculture of the time: wages, indebtedness, use of machinery, the productivity of fixed capital, labour productivity, international price movements. For all its massive array of statistics, this study teaches us next to nothing about the essential mechanisms of feudal exploitation by the landlords, the mainspring of Chinese rural economy of the period. Those mechanisms can be scientifically described, but only through a *qualitative* analysis of the type carried out during the same period by the Chinese Communists who were then organizing peasant guerrilla warfare in the hills of South China, hundreds of kilometres from Buck's comfortable study, but in direct contact with the daily life of the peasantry.

In the United States today, the champions of quantitative history are outdoing themselves, especially the practitioners of the New Economic History and the 'cliometric' school. Everything is reduced to models, to diagrams, to computer programmes. An attempt is made to determine, on the basis of a certain number of 'variables', how the American economy would have developed if, for example, the railroads had not been built; or how the South would have evolved if the Civil War had not put an end to slavery. And there are people who take these parlour games seriously! According to Gramsci,

> History is not a mathematical calculation. It has no decimal metric system or numbered units, enabling us to add, subtract, multiply and divide, construct equations and find square roots. Quantity (the economic structure) turns into quality. It becomes an instrument in the hands of human beings — human beings whose value cannot

be reduced to their weight, their height, or to the mechanical energy
their nerves and muscles can generate. They count *selectively* in terms
of their mental qualities, their behavior, sufferings, acceptance and
rejection.*

This critique of quantification does not mean that it cannot at times
be a useful technique, depending on the problems dealt with. It would
be worthwhile – and why not with the use of computers? – to obtain
precise statistics concerning the number of people from each region of
France who died on the battlefield during the First World War. Then we
would see written in letters of blood certain truths that our Jacobins –
of the Right or the Left – refuse to recognize, namely the extremely
heavy tribute that the rural populations of Brittany, Occitania and
Corsica have paid to an aggressive, centralizing French imperialism. This
is a *real* question, reflecting the concrete concerns – growing out of
their current struggles – of the minority nationalities of continental
France.

On the basis of all these false assumptions – historical 'facts', primary
'sources' and secondary 'works', diachrony-synchrony, periodization –
the basic characteristics of the historian's rhetoric can be defined. They
are those of capitalism as a whole – which that rhetoric reflects and
supports.

In the first place, historical rhetoric is both technicist and profession-
alist. Historical knowledge is for specialists whose naïve professional pride
is constantly in evidence.

Such professional historians harbour a deep suspicion of the 'amateurs' who, in their turn, complain bitterly of being shunted aside. The
following passage from Daniel Guérin's *Les Luttes des classes sous la
première Republique* is a typical expression of their attitude:

> It is both the strength and weakness of historians to be understood
> only by other historians. In France today, history – 'serious' history –
> is the monopoly of academics and archivists. And the monopoly is
> partially justified. Only specialists with nothing else to do have
> enough time to go to the sources. The techniques of history –
> 'serious' history, again – protect it against the amateurs, against the
> bold synthesizers who were the bane of Mathiez [the most prominent
> academic historian of the French Revolution in the 1930s].... The
> professionals live, moreover, in the past and not, as they should, in
> both the past and the present *at the same time*. They forget that,
> after all, the events they relate are a mere slice of life, a life as
> tumultuous as that of today.... The revolutionary worker of the
> present would be in a much better position to understand the
> *sans culottes* of 1793 than all the academics and archivists put

* Gramsci, *Ecrits politiques*, vol. 1, Paris 1975.

together, if he didn't have to spend his time earning his daily bread and had ample access to the archives and libraries.

The historian's professional jargon is a kind of code. His vocabulary, it is true, does not match the outrageous obscurity of the semiologists or the social psychologists, but the fact remains that it is understandable best to other historians. For it is stuffed with allusions, implicit references, camouflaged quotations that the expert alone can appreciate. The French scholar, Michel de Certeau, has pointed out that the writings of the historian only *seem* to be written for the general public; in reality, they are intended for his 'peers'.

Footnotes — whose ritualistic formalism gives the teacher a golden opportunity to 'condition' his students — are a good example of this 'coded' language. Such notes enable the author to comment smugly on his own text, putting questions to himself, making remarks, citing examples. In the footnotes he finds a pigeon-hole for the information he was unable to fit into the body of his text but did not want to 'let go to waste'; through them he can clarify allusions or formulations that were chosen mainly for effect. Most of these notes are either unnecessary or could easily have been incorporated into the text, if it had been more lucidly written. This does not mean that a figure, a quotation, an important reference does not, from time to time, require a word of explanation or identification.

Nor does it mean — more generally speaking — that history has no need for a division of labour based on special qualifications. But what kind of division of labour? Towards what social ends is it directed?

In the second place, the historian's rhetoric is deeply *intellectualist*. History is regarded as a 'discipline', an autonomous activity of the mind, an isolated field of study. Historical knowledge supposedly develops through continuous internal progress as the historians' knowledge, wisdom, know-how and capacity for meditation expand from age to age. In Michel Foucault's *Archéologie du Savoir*, even the problem of discontinuity is studied in purely intellectual terms. In his view, it was through the movement of ideas, the new ideas of the philosophers and the linguists, that the historians in their turn became aware of the phenomena of discontinuity. Not a word about people's struggles and the forces that bring about social change.

Lastly, the historians's rhetoric is *productivist*. It is necessary to *produce* — and at a merciless rhythm. This very real, though implicit, indoctrination, which comes to us from the United States — 'Publish or perish!' they say on the American campuses — is now universally accepted. So the historian is caught up in a swirl of theses and other major projects, 'provocative' articles, various publications, contributions to conferences, symposia, seminars. This leads to increasing specialization within constantly refined sub-specialities which further subdivide every ten years. Professor So and So is known, for example, as a historian of Chinese agriculture under the Guomindang, or of the American railroads before the Civil War.

Productivity is an end in itself, for historical knowledge operates as a closed system; it is *cumulative*. Every subject of research is equally 'valid', on the following conditions: (1) that it corresponds to a 'gap' in our knowledge (for in the minds of many academics, world history is a gigantic checkerboard on which every 'empty space' must be filled); (2) that 'duplication' be avoided as much as possible, for the same reasons; (3) that it can be discussed in the currently fashionable terminology; (4) that it can be approached with the help of material that is sufficiently abundant but preferably hard to reach. In other words, the way a subject fits technically into the existing pattern of knowledge is far more important than its real social function and the issues it raises. The thesis-machine must go on turning at all costs.

Thus, professionalism, technicism, unmitigated intellectualism, productivism — all serve and reinforce the Establishment, the basic values of the capitalist system and the entire prevailing ideology. The historian's rhetoric only deepens the gap between the masses and the specialists. The more the model of highly technical industrialized production is perfected, the more people are excluded, converted as everywhere else into passive consumers. In this way, the historian's rhetoric reinforces the intellectual's claim to play a special social role based on 'disinterested' knowledge and isolated from the people's struggles — except when they occasionally offer their moral support by signing 'appeals' and making speeches. This rhetoric also strengthens the productivist ideology of 'growth'. In their own special field, then, the historians help to keep the machine of the existing society in operation.

The collusion between the conventional historian's rhetoric and the power structure is particularly marked in the case of relations between 'advanced' and dependent countries. The downfall of the formal colonial regimes did not reduce, but rather intensified, the dependence of most of the Third World countries on the former ruling power. This neocolonialism is exercised in the field of historical studies no less than in more visible areas. Historians of the dependent countries are influenced to accept unresistingly the rhetoric of the Western world's historians by a series of considerations, such as the prestige of 'advanced' science, the eagerness of the formerly colonized to make an impression on their European 'masters'; implicit indoctrination, the orientation of historical studies in the newly independent countries in terms of the Western model, the temptation to shine in various Western university institutions such as international conferences, study missions, etc. The Western historian's rhetoric, skilfully presented as 'universal' and 'advanced', is an instrument of alienation for the intellectuals of the dependent countries, especially those from Black Africa.

> With the capitalist industrialization of Quebec, a more enlightened and less clerical élite set out to revise our past. Under cover of 'objective' scientific research, of 'historical' facts, historians from French-Canadian universities accumulated a great many 'facts' and historical documents. But their work went no further. According to them our history is one long unburial implicitly confirming our defeat and our subjection. In borrowing from the Americans their research methods, they also borrowed their point of view — the supremacy of the American capitalist system and the marginality of the little peoples, those remnants of another age.*

In the eyes of many, it is their 'scientific' claim, their ability to meet 'scientific' standards, that alone justifies the false bases of historical knowledge, such as quantification, positivism, periodization, the primacy of sources. Scientific accuracy — a concern for exactness, respect for reality, making sure of the facts, objective knowledge, the search for principles, connections and laws — is one thing. It is quite another to insist that the demands of scientific discipline can be achieved only through the prevailing technicist model for the expansion of knowledge as it exists today in the developed capitalist countries.

The essential criterion of scientific knowledge remains the two-way relationship between theory and practice. And this is something that history, by definition, can achieve only through *contact with the present*. Nobody would care to deny that the aim of history is the attempt to know the past. But what is meant by 'knowing'? We know a pear, said Mao, when we eat it — in other words, when we transform it through an *active relationship*. Obviously, knowing the past cannot mean acting on it directly. The knowledge of the past can only mean an active relationship to the world of today, which is its culmination. History is often called the 'science of the past', but it can be considered a science in the full sense of the term only if it avoids shutting itself up in the past. It is by analyzing, *in the first place*, our living society that general principles for the study of human societies, including those of the past, can be discovered. Such was the method used by Marx. The professional historians who are constantly talking about scientific accuracy but are unable to reach agreement concerning a scientific analysis of the present are either hypocritical or naive. They find it convenient, in any case, to turn their backs on the problems of their own society, at least in their 'professional work'. Other-

* L. Bergeron, *Petit Manuel de Québec*, preface.

wise, the false unity of the historian's rhetoric would break down in the university history departments, the editorial boards of scholarly periodicals, and innumerable conferences.

The prevailing model of historical rhetoric is neither infallible nor immutable. Many of the specialized works produced today on the basis of its false assumptions will some day be regarded as no less ridiculous, empty and spurious than those vast libraries of the seventeenth and eighteenth centuries with their hundreds of volumes devoted to subjects that have lost all semblance of reality for us today — for example, works on 'phlogistic', the imaginary substance of combustion, or heraldry, the 'science' of coats-of-arms. History has seen many examples of whole fields of knowledge becoming null and void, and will see many more in the future.

7 A sociological pocket-guide to historical knowledge

The Establishment's hierarchical structures – unofficial 'trusts' – Paris versus the provinces – semi-skilled workers and women – growth and departmentalism – USA–USSR – the attractions of history as merchandise – many are called, but few are chosen

The little world of professional historians obeys the 'laws of the milieu', to use Michel de Certeau's expression, and they are velvety but fierce. Its institutional structures are rigid and hierarchical, 'French-style'. Its range includes, for example, the elementary school teacher who 'dabbles in history' from time to time, the prestigious professor at the Collège de France, the secondary school history teacher, the professor in a provincial university or one in the Paris suburbs. Promotion from one echelon to another is strictly controlled and subject to a series of quaint initiation ceremonies, or *rites de passage*. The main thing is the historian's power to confer the authoritative label on others and so enable them to take their place in the profession. A distinguished professor at the top of the academic hierarchy can arrange a 'splendid career' for one of his 'pets' only if the person in question has the required diplomas and some 'impressive' publications to his credit. But these diplomas and writings have absolutely no value taken on their own – they are the administration's condition for the appointment from above to take place.

The system is particularly cruel to 'amateurs'. School teachers like Maitron or Dommanget have known this from experience – the aristocrats of the profession have consistently restricted them to subordinate or marginal positions, despite their outstanding contributions to French social history. And French students will never have the opportunity to benefit from the teaching of 'free-lancers' in history like Daniel Guérin, C. Manceron, H. Guillemin, B. Charbonneau. They are lucky if the works of these authors are even included in the university bibliographies, accompanied perhaps by a discreet warning.

Professional endogamy further increases the cohesion of historians as a social group. Most of the intraprofessional marriages originated when the budding historians were students together – two can face up better than one to the social and sexual solitude so typical of the university world. The career marriages are on a more sophisticated level. All doors open for the son-in-law of the 'big boss'. But the wife's maiden name is *never* included in the *curriculum vitae* that means so much in the profession — it is good taste to pretend to ignore this particular avenue to success. For the 'son', however, it is the royal road to the top of the hierarchy.

In the historian's profession, as in every other sector of academic life in France, the power structure is extremely rigid. The official institutional mechanisms give enormous authority to the 'mandarins', an authority that is magnified a hundred-fold by exercise and use. Through a series of complex, and typically French, administrative mechanisms, the most influential academic historians are in complete control of the appointment and promotion of other university teachers as well as of research funds. A historian has no other way of making himself known, of 'promoting' himself and his work, in the commercial sense of the term, than through publications in specialized periodicals or collections, papers read at the boring meetings of scholarly associations, participation in national or international conferences and seminars, scholarships and missions sponsored by prestigious foreign institutions. All these outlets are in the hands of the mandarins who control the main periodicals, the scholarly collections, the executive boards of specialized associations, the sponsoring committees for conferences and seminars. (All the details, of course, are taken care of by earnest neophytes.) Only after innumerable intrigues can a historian succeed in getting an article published in the *Revue Historique* or the *Annales,* in being chosen to participate in an illustrious international meeting, or in being sent to Harvard or Moscow. And the long waits, the disappointed hopes! The whole career of the would-be researcher, his moral satisfactions and material well-being alike, depend entirely on these promotion mechanisms, these financial sources, these avenues to success — and on the powers-that-be at the top of the pyramid.

The impact of the historical Establishment has recently been extended to the mass media where distinguished figures of the academic world have won important positions. They can display their talents and accomplishments by producing substantial works for the commercial publishers, participating in radio and television broadcasts, acting as influential and well-paid 'advisers', giving interviews to the newspapers. The young historian can share in these gratifying activities only if he enjoys the favour of the profession's leading figures who occupy strategic positions linking the university with the media.

The prevalent tension between Paris and the provinces of France extends to the little world of the historians. At one pole stands the capital, the seat of centralized power where national decisions are made concerning funds and appointments, and where the major publishers and research institutions are located. An eminent provincial professor is insignificant unless he carries weight within the decision-making centres in Paris. But in the recent period, the Paris-province relationship has become more complicated. Life in the provinces is often more comfortable, less trying. There, cooperation between the university and the local power structure is both more open and smoother. It is carried out mainly through Chambers of Commerce with an enthusiasm for regional history, local business groups and development commissions, the principal provincial newspapers and politicians, not to mention private interests in wine, for example, or real estate. It is no longer true that a 'splendid career' necessarily culminates in Paris.

The historical apparatus, like every organization of industrialized production, operates on the basis of a division of labour. It has its semi-skilled workers, its white-collar workers, its 'little bosses'. The numerical weight of this obscure labour force is constantly on the upswing. The historian who intends to 'produce' cannot do without a galaxy of research assistants, technical associates, administrative secretaries, etc. The narrower and more specialized the field of research, the stricter the division of labour. With no grasp of the end in view or the general meaning of the whole project in which he is involved, the semi-skilled worker in the history factory performs, passively and mechanically, a routine task such as searching through the archives, examining bibliographies, preparing and classifying material to be fed into the computers, working up statistics, etc. This underpaid labour force is supplemented by a reservoir of unpaid workers – the students who cut their teeth in historical methods by conducting research on topics of interest to their distinguished professor. Control over this inexhaustible supply of willing workers enables the 'big man' to expand his inventory of files at little expense to himself.

And it is invariably a *man*, for the world of the historians is deeply sexist. While the overwhelming majority of semi-skilled historical workers are women, their proportion rapidly dwindles at the higher echelons of the university hierarchy. Even among the lecturers, instructors and lower-level researchers, women are in a minority. They are almost non-existent at the top levels and are rarely to be found in any really influence-sharing post.

All these power structures contribute substantially to the growth of compartmentalized historical knowledge. To justify and maintain its existence, the institution must constantly expand, much like the capitalist factory whose mechanisms it reproduces and prolongs. A teacher asserts himself through his students, a research centre through its output. The subjects to be studied are chosen (or rather assigned) in terms of such considerations as the competitive situation in the field, the inclinations of the people running the institution, chances for promotion. As the British historians so neatly put it, there are certain particularly 'rewarding fields' — areas of study that yield tangible fruits by no means limited to the joys of disinterested knowledge. Here Parkinson's Law comes fully into play. Each sub-speciality immediately constitutes itself as a 'treasure field', strives to get organized and develop its own sphere of influence, keeping an eye out for the competition, standing guard at the borders to defend them from eventual attack. This is what has happened in the case of economic history, film history, Chinese history — all these specialities are a challenge to the traditional fields of the old-fashioned quadripartite scheme: Ancient Times, Middle Ages, Modern History, Contemporary History.

> So far as the university is concerned, the eighteenth century is a reserved area. Not because access to it is prohibited to outsiders, but because no one can enter it except after a long period of preparation and ceremonial rites. Eighteenth-century specialists who have managed to secure a research association, a periodical, statutes and conferences, enjoy a provisional right of exploitation over a part of the common field. Once the young scholar's thesis is completed, this option is converted into a property right.*

Growth and compartmentalization go together. An historian must be 'domiciled' — almost in the police sense of the word — in a specific sub-speciality, such as Byzantine history, for example, 'histoire des mentalités' in the sixteenth—eighteenth centuries, banking history, etc. Drifters, marginal elements, those without a fixed address, are suspect. As a result, the historian (with few exceptions) identifies more and more strictly with the institutions of his craft and all its power mechanisms as he rises from one year to the next in the academic hierarchy. Such an historian becomes *progressively* incapable of achieving an overview of the entire historical field and of grasping the relationship of the present and its problems to the living past. Although he continues to use the label, he is no longer an 'historian' in the general sense, but an 'historian-of-Greek-institutions' or an 'historian-of-the-labour-movement'. He is diminished like a shrunken head among the Amazonian Jivaros.

The above analysis is based on the situation in France, but it is equally applicable to the other major 'developed' countries. Historical studies in the United States are also characterized by a professional hierarchy, the exclusion of amateurs, rigid power structures, and an unequal division of labour. Even a great historian like Charles Beard was classified as an 'amateur' and boycotted for thirty years. The real power

*P. Chartier, 'Le XVIII Siècle, existe-t-il?' in *Le XVIIIe Siècle*, No. 5.

is exercised by the eminent names of the 'Ivy League', that occult coalition of the oldest universities, namely Harvard, Yale, Princeton, Columbia, Cornell. These figures dominate the allpowerful American Historical Association which makes and breaks careers through its annual conventions, commonly known as the 'slave market', where most of the university positions are more or less negotiated. In the United States, a thesis that does not involve extensive use of the computer is unacceptable in the university and many a career is based on the claim of doing 'original work' in some microscopic sub-speciality of the historical field.

The same hierarchical structure, the same productivist priorities, the same concentration of academic powers, the same intrigues around leading figures, the same clan rivalries — all this characterizes the Soviet historical profession, except that such phenomena are intensified there by the existence of a state bureaucracy enjoying a complete monopoly. The aptitude of the director of an Institute of the Academy of Sciences, or of an *otdel* (section), to become a full-fledged member of the Academy and thus win his way to the top of the hierarchy is decisive for the entire body of researchers in his Institute or *otdel*. This bureaucratic structure of the historical profession — reinforced by the strict separation between research (restricted to the Institutes of the Academy of Sciences) and teaching (restricted to the university) — was extended to the People's Democracies and to China in the 1950s. It is no accident that the Chinese history institutes, organized on the Soviet model, were immediately disbanded during the Cultural Revolution in 1966.

The social milieu of the professional historian is anything but neutral. Like the ideology of historical knowledge, it operates in complete conformity with the capitalist social order. There may be historians who consider themselves 'Left' as individuals, but the system is intimately linked to the Establishment, which it both *reflects* and *supports*. In the field of historical studies, it contributes to the maintenance of social relations based on money and profit, on the exploitation of subordinate workers — the basic characteristics of capitalist society!

And yet, those historians whose rhetoric is based on the critique of capitalism — in other words, those who are close to academic Marxism or identify with it — have never really challenged either the collusion between the history Establishment and the existing social order or that between the historian's conventional rhetoric and the ideology of the capitalist class.

All these power mechanisms are expanded by the recent commercialization of history, by the success of 'history-as-merchandise' among publishers, film producers, tourist promoters, radio and television directors. 'It sells well!' was the way an eminent 'left-wing' British university historian — who knows what he is talking about! — recently expressed it in the columns of the *Times Literary Supplement.*

Historical knowledge has become an article of commerce in the consumer's society. A new social type — the salesman of historical merchandise — has appeared on the scene. This new-style Gaudissart — a slightly modernized version of that character from a Balzac novel — is a go-getter with plenty of business sense and selling ability. He works closely with the social-climber types, the ambitious and complacent Rastignacs — another Balzacian character — of the academic world, who have managed to work their way into positions of influence. The historical series the publishers propose through these new literary brokers bring the academic historians interesting new outlets that spell not only cash but also prestige, as well as possible markets for their favourite students. Such series multiply like so many brands of biscuits or transistor-radios. In the main, they are supplied not by professional writers, but by academic historians who in this way find a profitable way of marketing their course material, their specialized research, various unused leftovers and waste matter from other works. There is a flowering of what the American publishers call 'non-books' — collections of articles by various authors on a particular theme, or of many articles by the same author on several themes, new editions of ancient texts, collections of selected material with extensive notes and comments — and the cleverest operators manage to combine several of these formulas.

What this all means is that the academic is *paid twice for the same work*: first, by the community since in France the professional historian draws his regular full-time salary as a 'teacher-researcher' — a bread-and-butter formula cherished by the French teachers' unions. Then the products of his teaching and research are marketed a second time in the private sector where they bring in the usual 10 per cent in royalties. I myself have played this game along with my 'dear colleagues'.

The result is inflation. The same specialist is solicited to work for several competing or complementary series and he constantly refurbishes and resells the same material, decked out somewhat differently each time — as the quality of his work gradually deteriorates.

For history books have been selling well, and may continue to do so unless and until this sector, too, is affected by the vicissitudes of the economy — increases in the price of paper, for example, or a market slump. The profession itself guarantees the historians a comfortable outlet through university study-programmes, the demand for new text-books, the desire of former students to 'keep abreast'. At the same time, the general public finds history books more readable and less obscure than genuinely scientific works or the more imaginative examples of the 'new novel'.

In addition to history books, there is a whole series of other market possibilities for the historian's merchandise — the mass-circulation press, films, guided tours for jaded travellers, 'Son et Lumière' shows, the reconstruction of historical landmarks. In the United States, the town of Williamsburg, Virginia, was restored to resemble what it was in pre-Revolutionary War days with its quaint buildings, workshops, costumes, arts and crafts — all for the benefit of the tourist trade. Here historical knowledge becomes just another gimmick, intended for pure entertainment and without the slightest social significance. But this apparently marginal aspect is an integral part of the new history industry.

This whole system of power, prestige and money that permeates the existence of the professional historian is both fiercely selective and mercilessly restrictive. It is based on a merciless process of selection. Even after managing to plant their feet solidly on the bottom rung of the academic hierarchy, how many will ever really 'succeed', from either the academic or the commercial point of view? How many will ever become star-historians on television, best-selling authors or distinguished professors? The others — the vast majority who will never 'make it' — wear themselves out uselessly or vegetate under the shadow of the big names, without succeeding, or even trying, to escape the clutches of the system — a system that has no tolerance for dissidence, criticism or nay-saying. Its mechanisms, despite their apparent flexibility, are unyielding, and in the end nobody — except the few who break away individually like the drop-outs of the American universities — can escape its complex network of compromise and complicity, so all-encompassing that it finally becomes accepted as part of the environment. The system draws much of its strength from its power of identification — the individual assimilates the social mechanisms of historical knowledge, interiorizes them to the point where they become an aspect of his personality. Is there any means of escape?

8 The traps of quadripartition in history

*A typically French systematization − crystallization of the history
bureaucracy and Eurocentrism − the specific historical function of
'ancient, medieval, modern and contemporary' history − the intellectual
and political bankruptcy of quadripartism − academic Marxism cannot
resuscitate it*

In France, the study and teaching of history as a discipline integrated
into the academic apparatus are divided into four large sections supposedly
corresponding to the division of historical time:

■ *Ancient History:* In reality, this is the history of Ancient Greece and
Rome with a glance at the Egypt of the Pharaohs and the Assyrian and
Babylonian empires. This period conventionally extends to the fall of the
Roman Empire, dated from the capture of Rome by the barbarians in
AD 410 or the fall of the Western Roman Empire in AD 484.

■ *The Middle Ages:* This means essentially the Western Middle Ages,
with a brief examination of Byzantium, Eastern Europe and the Arab
countries of the Mediterranean. The period in question extends to the
capture of Byzantium by the Turks in 1453 and to the discovery of
America by Columbus in 1492.

■ *Modern History:* This too is centred on Europe, including its colonial
extensions overseas. This period goes up to the French Revolution (using
either 1789, 1799 or 1815 as the cut-off date).

■ *Contemporary history:* This is the only area in which an effort is made
to go beyond the European framework and take a real interest in the
countries of Asia, Africa and America.

It should be stressed from the outset that this quadripartite arrangement of world history is specifically French. In other countries, the past
is organized differently, in terms of other reference-points. In Greece,
for example, Ancient Times extends to the fifteenth century, and the
Turkish occupation represents a kind of Middle Ages. In China, 'modern'
history (*jindai*) extends from the Opium Wars to the patriotic movement
of May 1919, which marks the beginning of 'contemporary' history
(*jiandai*). In the United States, national history is divided into three main
sections on the basis of several decisive watersheds, such as the War of

Independence at the end of the eighteenth century and the Civil War.

But it is perhaps in France that the systematization of world history into a rigid quadripartite structure is carried to extremes. Quadripartition fulfils definite functions both ideologically and at the level of academic institutions. It serves as an official ideological apparatus.

■ *Its pedagogical function:* These four broad sections provide the framework for the history programmes in the secondary schools as well as in the universities, which implies a similar orientation for the textbooks and historical series.

■ *Its institutional function:* Quadripartition also governs the distribution of teaching posts in the universities. And the specialized agencies that control research funds and appointments in the academic world are also organized along quadripartite lines. It is around these same broad sections that the academic cliques crystallize. For example, the teachers of Ancient History and of the History of the Middle Ages are sufficiently influential in the French Ministry of Education to make sure that their respective sections each accounts for a third of the history curriculum leading to the special *agrégation* diploma required for teaching in the secondary schools. This naturally results in a guarantee of students, assistants, funds, etc. And yet, the whole history of the world up to the sixteenth century represents, justifiably, only a small proportion of the teaching the future graduate will be expected to provide his secondary school pupils.

■ *Its intellectual function:* Quadripartition is the basis of the division of labour in historical research, and the four main sections are so many airtight subsections. There are, of course, other criteria, other ways of dividing up the historical field and marking out areas of specialization. The historian can be a specialist on a particular country or a special aspect of social experience – religious history, economic history, the history of ideas, etc. Except for a few marginal cases, however, these sub-specialities lack legitimacy and respectability. They are not generally regarded as meeting the standards of scientific history unless they are pursued within one of the four basic sectors – the economic history of ancient Greece, the history of commerce in the Middle Ages, modern demographic history, to cite a few examples.

■ *Its ideological and political function:* The end result of this quadripartition is to overestimate the role of the West in world history, and underestimate both qualitatively and quantitatively the place of the non-European peoples in human development. From this standpoint, quadripartition is an integral aspect of the intellectual apparatus of imperialism. To the vast majority of mankind, the events regarded as so decisive – such as the fall of the Roman Empire, the capture of Byzantium – mean little. The choice of these events also emphasizes the history of political superstructures, of states – a preference that is not without ulterior motives.

The specific ideological function of quadripartition is to give an anchoring in the past to certain cultural values that are essential to the ruling bourgeoisie. Thus, ever since the Renaissance, and even more since the French Revolution, the history of Greece and Rome has been regarded, for political reasons, as one of the foundations of bourgeois culture in France. It was not so long ago that students were expected to compose verses in Latin at the Baccalaureat examinations and to defend their doctoral theses in Latin – as Jean Jaurès did! A knowledge of Greek or Latin was an unmistakable sign of membership in the ruling class – and this situation changed only recently with the new predominance of mathematics.

The ideological character of the Middle Ages is no less marked. It is a deeply Christian period and provides many an occasion to exalt the values of 'Christian civilization', such as the family, royalty, the crusades, chivalry – a whole persistent vocabulary. In the original meaning of the term itself, the concept of the Middle Ages is ideological. It is conceived, according to Bloch, as 'an intermediary age between the Incarnation that brought an end to the Old Law and the blessed day of the long-awaited Kingdom of God.' Making the Middle Ages one of the basic categories of world history means perpetuating the prestige and predominance of conservative Catholic circles and the Church; the 'Christian civilization' they claim to inherit is set up as one of the four pillars of Time itself.

Pompidou, the lay school-teacher's son who joined the camp of the upper bourgeoisie, consistently played his role of ideological defender of the Establishment by restoring Latin in the Lycée curriculum and by organizing massive festivities in 1970 in honour of Saint Louis, King of France, seven centuries after his death.

Since the days of Voltaire, at any rate, the term Modern Times has consecrated the claim of the rising bourgeoisie to bring an end to history, and – in the name of its 'modernism' – to control the future of all mankind. For the past dozen or so years, 'modern' history has been separated from 'contemporary' history within the institutional structures of the university but it still plays a specific ideological role. The period of the fifteenth to the eighteenth century is portrayed as the Golden Age of the *anciens régimes*, especially those whose more flexible political mechanisms seemed to enable them to avoid revolutions or at least reduce them to mere accidents along the way. So that period has become the favourite choice of the 'long view' school, the partisans of a history that is massive in scope and in fact de-politicized. From this standpoint, the study of demographic problems, of ideas, of technological development, of popular or erudite culture, can be carried on smoothly, undisturbed by such nuisances as mass political struggles, crises or sudden upheavals. In the study of this 'modern' period, historians of the Right or Far Right who are in love with pre-capitalist society, and 'left-wing' historians who are enthusiasts of the New History, make comfortable bedfellows on the basis of a political compromise designed precisely to eliminate the political dimension of history.

The 'contemporary age', the fourth pillar of the historical edifice, conveys an equally definite ideological message: the West's vocation to become the political and economic master of the entire world. Non-European history – relegated to a marginal, exceptional role in the other three sections – is an essential and integral part of this ideological offensive; its right to exist is uncontested within the historical profession. The West's mastery over the earth is expressed in the ability of Western historians to draw up a coherent, global picture of the nineteenth- and twentieth-century world and thus to assume leadership of African, Asian or American destiny.

Yet this quadripartite scheme is intellectually inadequate even for Europe and in terms of the conventional historian's own rhetoric. It artificially slices up various original and homogeneous areas of history, such as the history of the maritime region of the Baltic and North Seas between the thirteenth and eighteenth centuries, with its string of major commercial cities stretching from Amsterdam to Riga that still bear a family resemblance. Quadripartition also relegates to the background some of the most interesting phenomena, the deepest mutations and historical watersheds. Specialists on the 'Later Roman Empire' or the 'Early Middle Ages' are authoritatively assigned to distinct sections of the historical apparatus; they are confined to one side of the border or the other and so prevented from making a really thorough study of the pivotal period that straddles Ancient Times and the Middle Ages. Quadripartition also interferes with the study of specific long-range phenomena such as the village community, the role of utopia, unconventional warfare, marginal social groups, etc. The result is a form of real indoctrination. The historian finally convinces himself that his competence must be confined to one of the officially approved basic categories and he refrains from any attempt at general or comparative thinking.

But this quadripartism is belied by the march of history itself. It cannot account for developments in the contemporary world or answer the demands of the present. To begin with, it reflects a Eurocentrism that is increasingly ridiculous. The world of the White Man – of the WASPS (White Anglo-Saxon Protestants) – is coming to an end. Nixon had to go to Canossa – i.e., to China – to pay homage to Mao and climb up on the Great Wall. Saigon and Phnom-Penh have been liberated by peasant armies that stood up against the world's greatest power; and, in the United Nations, the industrialized countries of the West that completely dominated the League of Nations a half-century ago have been reduced to a minority.

At the same time, as Zhou En-lai pointed out, 'we live in a world of nations.' The problems of national identity completely overshadow the vast schemes of conventional history. And quadripartism, in the last analysis, turns out to be just one more version — and not necessarily the best — of the old dream of a 'discourse on world history'. It has been shaken like the dream itself.

In any case, history conceived as the knowledge of a world external to ourselves is now forced to redefine itself as a *dynamic* relationship to the past. Social practice breaks down the airtight compartments of quadripartition and unifies the historical field in terms of its own priorities. Denouncing the contemporary penal system, for example, means thinking seriously about that institution from a long-range viewpoint, irrespective of the usual categories of 'medieval' or 'modern' history. And the militants of the women's liberation movement are examining, intensely and effectively, such problems as the original subjugation of their sisters, the 'cave-women', or the specific new types of social exploitation introduced by the Industrial Revolution.

Must Marxist theory come to the rescue of an outdated quadripartism? Must the latter be given a new lease of life through the concept of a succession of basic modes of production, with Ancient History corresponding to slavery, the Middle Ages to feudalism, Modern Times to rising capitalism and the contemporary period to developed capitalism already confronted — ever since the victory of the Russian Revolution in 1917 and of the Chinese Revolution in 1949 — by the new reality of socialism.

There is no denying that the modes of production are powerful historical forces. Each one imparted a definite structure to the social fabric through the unity of the economic base with the superstructure. Throughout the Middle Ages, the basic characteristics of the feudal system of production put their mark on the family, moral values, the writing of history, the division of labour among crafts, the practice of diplomacy, etc. — for all these aspects of social experience are deeply integrated into the feudal reality. At the same time, the principles of Marxist social analysis make possible a more meaningful interpretation of Ancient Rome or early capitalism, from every point of view.

But the basic modes of production as defined by Marx are a *typology*, a contribution to the *theory* of social structures. They represent significant *extreme cases* which are fully realized only in certain very specific historical situations — in Ancient Greece or Rome, for example, though not throughout the entire Roman Empire; under the feudal regimes of Western Europe between the eleventh and fourteenth centuries; or in North America since the middle of the nineteenth century. Hardly a sufficient basis for the reconstruction, along the old quadripartite lines, of a 'discourse on world history', updated by Marxism.

9 The historian's nostalgia for 'history in the grand style'

The existing system as the end result of human development – world history as a 'marketing operation' – various attempts at a general interpretation of world history – Althusser, sugar and history

There is a strong temptation among historians to develop a general 'discourse on world history'. The expression is from Bossuet, but the attempt was also made by Herodotus in his *Histories,* by Saint Augustine in his *City of God,* by Ibn Khaldun in his *Mukaddima,* by Otto of Freising, by Voltaire in his *Essai sur les moeurs,* by Hegel, by Toynbee, by a UNESCO team after the Second World War.

The main object of such a 'discourse on world history' is to present a logical, analytical view of the entire course of human development, showing how the succession of great historical periods leads inevitably to the age in which the author is privileged to live. From this standpoint, the present society, viewed as the culmination of all world history, is amplified and legitimized by its position in time. Bossuet used this approach when he reduced the course of past centuries to a slow but sure advance toward the Absolute Monarchy of the Very Christian King, Louis XIV. Voltaire used an approach that was identical in content though opposite in form when he wrote the *Essai sur les moeurs* to glorify the progressive character of the eighteenth-century 'Age of Enlightenment' – a period that was little more, in reality, than a precarious cultural compromise between the aspirations of the rising bourgeoisie and the political inertia of the *ancien régime.*

Toynbee's approach is no different. In his series, *A Study of History,* he sketches a typology and framework for the world's nineteen major 'civilizations'. The collective work of six fat volumes, undertaken by UNESCO in the aftermath of the Second World War and entitled *A History of the Cultural and Scientific Development of Mankind,* amounts to a massive plea for a kind of apolitical, cosmopolitan culturalism as the way out of the crises of our time. The historic responsibilities of the various economic power structures for the tragedies of the twentieth century – its wars and political repression, especially the role of Nazi Germany — are implicitly relegated to the background. The 'World History' series produced in abundance in the Soviet Union these days (*mirovnaia istoriia*) have a similar didactic, ideological function. They are written in strict conformity with the 'five-stage theory' and are imbued with the same spirit of dogmatic, mechanical Marxism. Their effect is to glorify the existing Soviet society as the pinnacle of world history. In these thick volumes, Marxism is reduced to a technical instrument for the ordering — *Einordnung,* as the academic Marxists of East Germany say — of past societies; it is no longer in any real sense a 'guide to action'.

There are still other, much inferior, examples of this 'discourse on world history', such as the numerous works along these lines that have been published ever since the nineteenth century. Though seemingly commercial, their ideological content — less explicit perhaps than in the major undertakings mentioned above — is quite definite. They are expensive and ornamental, usually produced in fancy bindings and profusely illustrated. The artistry of their production takes precedence over the quality of the text itself. All this art-work and technique tends to *reify* the human past, to convert it into a luxurious piece of merchandise completely irrelevant to the live issues of today's society. When the executive or dignitary lines up these handsome volumes along the shelves of his living-room, he asserts almost physically his own claim — and that of his social class — to mastery over world history. At his fingertips are the gropings of the Sumerians toward science, the mysterious Mayas, the conquests of the Byzantine, Sassanid and Mongol empires, the adventures of the great explorers, the revolutions of modern times, the two World Wars. From his comfortable armchair, he contemplates and dominates all this — even if he has not actually read all the books on his shelves! His feeling of mastery is perhaps tempered with a touch of scepticism and fashionable relativism. 'It has all happened so many times before!' 'History proceeds by cycles!' 'Change is only superficial!' The commercialized historical series are politically demobilizing.

In this age of multinational marketing, such ventures are all the more profitable when carried out with the collaboration of historians of various nationalities. In this way, an 'equal balance' can be maintained among the histories of different countries. Care is taken to reach the widest, most varied public, which means that anything more or less offensive or disturbing is prudently trimmed. To reach this cosmopolitan market, arrangements are made from the outset for translations — or better yet, the books are published jointly in different countries. Larousse, Fischer, Weidenfeld and Nicolson, La Pléiade and many others are accustomed to operations of this sort, and the strictly commercial imperatives of such ventures are also deeply ideological. For this multinational historical merchandise implies, by definition, the rejection of any trace of national identity, of relevance to current problems, and therefore of the slightest link between past and present. Here an active relationship to the past is out of the question.

As a reaction against this encyclopaedic approach to history and the purely factual description of the past, historians have been making an effort to think in a more general way. Such rethinking concerns the entire course of world history and is on a somewhat higher level that what we have been describing. This 'discourse on world history' of a more sophisticated sort has developed in several main directions:

- The *philosophy of history,* or theoretical and philosophical considera-
tion of the content and meaning of human history. This has been with us for a long time – examples of it are the writings of Jean Bodin and G. B. Vico at the beginning of Modern Times, then the work of Monte-squieu and Volney in the eighteenth century, of Herder, Hegel and John Stuart Mill in the nineteenth century, of Croce, Carr, and Raymond Aron in the twentieth.
- *Historical methodology,* or the analysis of techniques of historical research. The outstanding names in this field are Collingwood and Namier, Langlois and Seignobos, Samaran and Marrou. Is history a science? What are its analytical procedures and principles? These are the questions to which those historians address themselves.
- *Comparative history,* or the parallel analysis of two or three analogous 'cases' of the same phenomenon in the past. British and Japanese feudal-ism, for example, are choice subjects for the specialists of comparative history. Roland Mousnier examined the peasant uprisings of the seven-teenth century as they occurred in France, in Russia and in China. The University of Chicago periodical, *Comparative Studies in Society and History,* takes this approach. As a rule, it amounts to a mere juxta-position of monographs, linked by some remarks of a general nature.
- *Historiography,* or the rational description of the successive stages of historical knowledge. These stages are viewed as the continuous, cumula-tive development of such knowledge as it rises to the level of a 'genuine science'. The accent is always on the 'progress' of historical knowledge rather than on its specific political role in any particular society.

In France, these four approaches developed (with only a few excep-tions) much later than in Germany, Italy or the English-speaking countries. The French historians – who had long been resting on their professional laurels (Robert Mandrou wrote, in the *Encyclopédia Universalis,* of their 'unjustified good conscience') – suddenly realized that their brand image would suffer unless they made an effort to analyze the specific content of their discipline. As a result, there has recently been a flowering of works with theoretical pretensions under the signature of certain well-known historians. But this belated output adds nothing to the many earlier works produced in other countries on the same general themes of historical knowledge. They fail to transcend its conventional false assumptions and accept unquestioningly its intellectualism, its technicism, its productivism. The outstanding exception, of course, is Bloch's *Apologie,* which is in a class by itself. This earlier work was a precursor. Written under political and personal circumstances that no academic has experienced since, it represents a pathetic compromise between Bloch's 'old self', the distinguished dignitary that he never repudiated in himself and, on the other hand, the unprecedented situation he faced at the time of writing when he was driven from his university as a Jew and hunted down by the police. It is no accident that I have borrowed so lavishly from the *Apologie,* quoting it frequently to make even contradictory points — for example, to illustrate the typically professional attitude toward the 'historian's trade' and, at other times, to emphasize his efforts to let in new intellectual light, come to grips with the present, speak in the first person singular, question his own role.

Louis Althusser wanted to go further. His essay, 'Sur le concept d'histoire' (*La Pensée*, June 1965), is worth reading. The classics of Marxism may be intensely steeped in historical references, but not one has tried to provide a general theoretical analysis of the past-present relationship. In Althusser's case, there is an attempt to break with what he calls 'the religious dreams of the communion of the Saints and the resurrection of the dead' in the Michelet style — in other words, with history's claim to 'reconstruct the past', to accumulate, as if it were an end in itself, the greatest possible amount of coherent information about the past. The historian's real task, he suggests, is to reflect on history but not as if it were a general Idea in the Hegelian sense; it is to analyze 'the specific structures of historicism peculiar to each mode of production.'

So far, so good. Althusser's arguments and formulations are a useful contribution to a radical critique of the historian's professional rhetoric — for a reconstructionist like Michelet, or perhaps a Cuvier, lies dormant in many a historian. What an ambitious project it is to reconstruct the past from its sparse fragments! What a challenge to merciless time! No less fruitful is Althusser's suggestion of a specific historical approach for each type of society. As a matter of fact, the internal development of capitalism displays its own particular rhythms, unparalleled by the rhythms of previous societies: technological breakthroughs (such as the electricity, atomic and computer 'revolutions'), the play of discontinuity in world crises and world wars, chain effects of planetary scope. The dynastic cycles of strong power structures, of peasant revolts, of foreign invasions — all reveal a characteristic rhythm in the 'Asiatic' societies. Wars of conquest, that inexhaustible source of slaves, constitute the framework of the history of the slave society. The feudal society — where power is based on land and therefore on its acquisition by war, inheritance or diplomacy — is also punctuated by wars and conquest.

But Althusser strives to go further into abstraction. In his view, the real aim of history is 'not to know what has happened *in* history but how the concept of history has been produced in its most specific features'. All this, of course, remains extremely intellectual. Althusser even goes so far as to write: 'The knowledge of history is *no more historical* than the knowledge of sugar is sugary.' A surprisingly weak sophism, implying a rejection of the entire Marxist contribution, particularly the definition of science, of scientific knowledge, as the combination of theory and practice. For sugar is incapable of communicating its own substance to the knowledge we have of it. But knowledge, including historical knowledge, is inseparable from the type of historical — and *necessarily historical* — society that produces it.

When Althusser escapes into the 'concept of history', or when — as in his response to John Lewis — he accuses history of being a science without an aim, he squelches a basic question: Who makes history? In the name of conceptualization, he takes refuge in the mechanistic theory that the productive forces make history, that they determine the main contradictions of society. This sounds like a Marxist version of that 'history in the grand style' so fashionable at the moment. These two convergent approaches agree in denying a leading role to the masses of people. During a debate organized by the *Annales,* Pierre Vilar rightly replied to Althusser that it is men who make history and in doing so assert mastery over their own future. World history is not the subject of a discourse — however theoretically sophisticated — but the stake in a struggle.

10 Pre-capitalist societies: have they a common past?

The fascination of long-distance connections in the age of affluence – very old roots – empires, migrations, large-scale trade, technical exchanges, long-distance travel – the pre-capitalist societies had no structural need for such long-distance exchanges

It is one thing to resist the intellectual temptation to indulge in an encyclopaedic 'discourse on world history'; it is quite another to examine the relations that have linked various peoples, various human societies, throughout the course of history. This is a genuine problem, and our own age looks backwards to history in the hope of finding an answer to it. Throughout the twentieth century, and especially in the 1970s, we have been intensely aware of a contradiction between the specific identities of each people and the growing tendency towards global independence among all human groups.

According to Marx, world history – the common history of the various peoples – begins only with capitalism and the appearance of the international capitalist market. Up to the sixteenth century, the existence of a common history – even one rooted deeply in the past – was made impossible by the restrictions and isolation inherent in the earlier modes of production: slavery, feudalism and the 'Asiatic' system. Capitalism not only facilitated the emergence of such a common history, but also discovered in its underlying principles the basis for a global history propelled by certain common mechanisms.

Even before the rise of a world capitalist market, the destiny of human beings was determined by factors other than the internal development of the community to which they belonged, such as their people, city, tribe or empire. Their destiny was also shaped by a whole series of exchanges, contacts and long-distance influences.

The study of such relationships and influences is, and always has been, a fascinating one. In this age of nearly instantaneous travel from one end of the planet to the other and of widespread standardization of ways of living, through universal gadgetry and vast identical structures

of concrete and steel, the idea of contacts and exchanges that span the
centuries is both attractive and agonizing. But there is more involved
here than mere curiosity or a superficial taste for the exotic.

The widespread interest shown today for the pre-capitalist societies –
particularly those furthest removed from ourselves, such as the Sumerians, the Incas, the ancient Polynesians, the Dravidians – is the reflection of several definite needs:

■ Each people's desire to locate itself in historical time and to become
fully aware of its most ancient roots as a means of strengthening national
cohesiveness and asserting its collective identity. This is true of the
Australian Aborigines, the Vietnamese, the Mexicans, the Iranians, but
also for the Basques, the Corsicans, the Celts, who know that their
presence on what is today the territory of France goes back much
further than the Roman conquest or the Teutonic invasions.

■ The search for historical reference-points to give an extra dimension
to present currents of international exchange, especially those that by-
pass Europe and activate the international relations of the Third World,
despite the claims of the West to world hegemony. No longer do all
roads lead to Rome – if they ever did! While visiting Dar-es-Salaam,
Zhou En-lai hailed the ancient friendship between China and the peoples
of Africa, and referred to the recent discovery of some extremely old
Chinese pottery along the coasts of Tanzania.

■ The current interest in exploring past societies to find negative
images of our own society. Historical distance enables us to use the
experience of ancient peoples, so 'different' from ourselves, to bring
into sharp relief the essential characteristics of the contemporary world.

Space does not permit a systematic inventory of all the factors that
have contributed, since pre-capitalist times, to the establishment of a
history common to all the peoples of the earth. Such an inventory would,
in any case, easily fall prey to the pitfalls of encyclopaedism. A few
examples, however, should be mentioned:

■ *Political-military groupings:* The phenomenon of empires is one that
acutely preoccupied the rising bourgeoisie: Montesquieu, Volney, Gibbon
and others reflected at great length on the fall of the Roman Empire.
The rising class, with its ambition of inaugurating a new social order that
would be both universal and permanent, felt the need to identify the
circumstances and causes of the decline and fall of other regimes that
had started out with similar claims. The new ruling class wanted a more
secure future for itself.

All these empires – the Chinese, the Persian, the Egyptian, the Roman,
the Inca, the Byzantine, the German, the Mongol, the Mughal – were
built up through military conquest. They achieved a certain level of
politico-administrative stability and territorial integrity as expressed in

definite borders. Eventually they collapsed. But they still laid claim to universality in terms of their ideological principles rather than their territorial scope alone. The phenomenon of vast, relatively stable, imperial blocs was apparently common to the various pre-capitalist forms — slavery, 'Asiatic' and feudal.

Contrasting with these empires were the city-state archipelagos where each city, within a fairly homogeneous cultural and social area, was defined as a political absolute invested with divine rights. Examples of such entities were the cities of ancient Mesopotamia, of classical Greece, of pre-Angkor Cambodia, of the Mayan civilization, of medieval Italy, of the Baltic states (the Hansa).

■ *Cultural-religious systems,* such as the Greco-Roman world, the Confucian world, Hinduism, Buddhism, Islam, Christianity. These systems have occasionally coincided with more or less unified political-military entities — the Greco-Roman religion and the Roman Empire, Confucianism and the Chinese empire (along with the 'tributary' countries), the Arab empire of the first caliphs. Usually these religious systems, in the broad sense, covered a vaster area and lasted longer than the structures that supported them for a time or constituted their initial political nucleus. This is especially true for Buddhism. As for Islam, it spread not only to the Philippines but also to Senegal, to central Russia as well as to the archipelago of the Indian Ocean. Christianity made its presence felt, from the Middle Ages onwards, from Newfoundland to Central Asia and from Ethiopia to Scandinavia.

These great religious systems were spread through war, through the conversion of kings, and particularly through trade. They have proven capable of organizing an entire society, including the family, law, administration, literature. And they have often engaged in ruthless warfare that pitted them against one another — Christianity versus Islam in the Mediterranean area, for example, or Buddhism versus Hinduism in Indochina.

■ *Migrations* — Mass migrations constitute the very warp and woof of so-called 'proto-history' and account for the more or less definitive settlement of the Celts, Germans, Slavs in Europe as well as of most of the peoples of Central Asia, Indochina, Oceania and India. In more recent times, migrations continued to play a significant role, some examples being those of the Normans and the Hungarians in the European Middle Ages, of the Thais in Indochina, or of the Peuls in Western Africa well into modern times. So much for the long-distance mass migrations. The current distribution of major ethnic and linguistic groups also results from the migrations of various peoples, dispersions and 'diasporas', not only of the Jews but also of the Gypsies, the Armenians, the Lebanese, who are scattered over the five continents.

■ *Large-scale trade* – Long-distance exchanges are very ancient. Roman or Chinese money and pottery are spread widely throughout Europe, Asia and Africa and have been unearthed by excavations. The geographers of the ancient Mediterranean area traced four long commercial routes that penetrated deep into barbarian territory – for example, the 'tin route' leading to the mining islands of the Atlantic, the 'silk route' leading to Central Asia, the 'amber route' leading to the Baltic, the 'ivory route' leading to the Upper Nile and Central Africa.

Large-scale, long-distance trade in the pre-capitalist era necessarily involved non-perishable goods of high value in comparison with their weight, for transportation by land or water is costly. The articles traded were such irreplaceable items as tea, salt, medicines, etc., or luxury goods such as porcelain, varnish, ivory, skins, lacquer, etc. Supervision of such long-distance trade was one of the main functions of the 'Asiatic' state and a feature of its 'economic high command'. In the ancient African societies, such supervision constituted – in the absence of vast public works – the essential economic responsibility of the state.

■ *The circulation of techniques* – Specialists have been able to draw up detailed charts showing the types of sails used for navigation and their distribution in the world, the development of metallurgical techniques in Europe and Asia, the various types of writing, and of cultivated plants, in different parts of the world. From very ancient times, exchanges of techniques took place over considerable distances and often with great rapidity. Phoenician writing, in its various forms, spread not only throughout the Mediterranean, but all over the Middle East and as far as South-east Asia. Pre-capitalist China is often mentioned as an example of historical stagnation. And yet, only a few years after the Portuguese settled in Macao in the sixteenth century, so-called American-type crops – which the Portuguese had brought with them – were spread all over China: they included taro, yams, peanuts, tobacco. Such hardy plants made it possible to farm the sandy lands and the sloping earth that were unsuitable for irrigated rice-fields. China experienced a veritable 'green revolution'.

■ *Long-distance travel* – Marco Polo was not a unique case. In the Hellenistic period, travellers like Megasthenes and Cosmas Indicopleustes penetrated deep into Asia. In the fifteenth century, an Arab, Ibn-Battuta, not only visited the same countries of Asia as Marco Polo, but also vast areas of South Asia, the Middle East, Africa. The Vikings may have reached Canada as early as the tenth century. The Chinese explorer, Xuantang, went to India by way of the Himalayas in the seventh century and brought back the sacred Buddhist scriptures; another Chinese, Cheng Ho, reached the eastern coasts of Africa in the fifteenth century at the head of the Ming dynasty's imperial fleet.

The pre-capitalist societies, then, did not live in isolation. They experienced long-distance exchanges — and therefore genuine interdependence — in every branch of social life. But these relations were discontinuous, partial, even marginal. The empires rose and disintegrated. The adventures of the great explorers were hardly known at all and in any case soon forgotten. For such long-distance exchanges did not affect the basic economic structures, whether of the 'Asiatic', slave or feudal type. They were not *historically* necessary to the reproduction of those structures. The relations, once established, could easily evaporate, slip completely into oblivion, as happened in the case of the Northmen in Canada or the Chinese in Africa. Or they could simply run out of steam, mark time. Thus the Arabs, Indians, Chinese, successively approached the Australian coasts between the tenth and fifteenth centuries, but their contacts remained fragile and reversible. These explorers were not impelled by the fundamental economic imperatives of their social system to penetrate Australia and settle there.

On the other hand, the relationship the Westerners established with Australia in the era of capitalism was irreversible, for it was based on a structural necessity: capitalism's urge towards indefinite expansion with a view to the expanded reproduction of capital. And that is what Marx meant when he said that world history begins with the world capitalist market.

11 Capitalism:
the great unifier of history

*The expanded reproduction of capital is the basis of world history –
capitalism remakes the world in its own image – technological levelling,
migrations, world wars and world crises unify the planet – polarization
between rich countries and poor – the world village and the world city*

Capitalism is qualitatively distinct from the socio-economic systems that
preceded it, for it is based on both the *capacity* and the *necessity* for unlimited self-development. Capital, the foundation of the system, can
exist only by increasing its own substance; it must constantly be invested
in new activities generating more surplus-values and therefore more capital
requiring still further outlets. The imperatives of its internal dynamics
create for the system a field of action that extends to the ends of the
earth. One of the most famous passages of the *Communist Manifesto*
describes this global invasion in terms that sound as fresh today as when
they were written over a century ago:

> The need of a constantly expanding market for its products chases
> the bourgeoisie over the whole surface of the globe. It must nestle
> everywhere, settle everywhere, establish connections everywhere.
> The bourgeoisie has, through its exploitation of the world-market,
> given a cosmopolitan character to production and consumption in
> every country. To the great chagrin of reactionists, it has drawn from
> under the feet of industry the national ground on which it stood. All
> old-established national industries have been destroyed or are daily
> being destroyed. They are dislodged by new industries whose intro-
> duction becomes a life and death question for all civilized nations,
> by industries that no longer work up indigenous raw material, but raw
> material drawn from the remotest zones; industries whose products
> are consumed, not only at home, but in every quarter of the globe. In
> place of the old wants, satisfied by the productions of the country, we
> find new wants, requiring for their satisfaction the products of distant
> lands and climes. In place of the old local and national seclusion and
> self-sufficiency, we have intercourse in every direction, universal inter-
> dependence of nations. And as in material, so also in intellectual pro-
> duction. The intellectual creations of individual nations become com-
> mon property. National one-sidedness and narrow-mindedness become
> more and more impossible, and from the numerous and local literature
> there arises a world-literature.

> The bourgeoisie, by the rapid improvement of all instruments by production, by the immensely facilitated means of communication, draws all, even the most barbarous nations, into civilization. . . . It compels all nations, on pain of extinction, to adopt the bourgeois mode of production; it compels them to introduce what it calls civilization into their midst, i.e. to become bourgeois themselves. In a word, it creates a world after its own image.

In this sense, world history, the merging of each people's distinct history in a common destiny, truly began with the sixteenth century. This meant more than the geographic expansion of trade currents across the entire planet and the emergence of a world history in purely spatial terms. The history of each people was simultaneously transformed qualitatively through the operation of common unifying mechanisms – the world market orienting the production of each country in terms of its demands, its world prices, its world financial groups, from the time of the old East India Company to the giant 'multinationals' of today. All these factors contributed greatly to universalizing the very mechanisms of history and not its geographical field of action alone. This situation has not been modified even by the development of the socialist bloc before and after the Sino-Soviet split in 1960. The Socialist countries of Europe find themselves navigating, to an increasing extent, in the wake of Western capitalism; they eagerly seek its trade, react to its initiatives and stimulation, require its technological innovations and copy its pattern of consumption. China too realizes that, despite her proclaimed desire for self-sufficiency, she is still dependent on the capitalist world market as the dominant mode of production with its world raw-material prices, its financial mechanisms and its 'ready-made' factories. The reality of a common world history makes itself felt in every important sphere of social experience.

The world – including the most inaccessible continents and even the polar zones – has been completely explored. The planet has become a closed system, a fact clearly grasped by the great utopian socialist writers of the nineteenth century. Fourier was obsessed by the planetary dimension. Saint-Simon, and Enfantin after him, used to say: 'The globe alone is our fiancee, our mother!' Jules Verne followed the same line of thought and his *Voyages extraordinaires* are an epic expression of this bold planetary outlook.

Production techniques, consumer's goods, ways of living: all have become increasingly standardized. This is not the result exclusively of ruthless economic mechanisms, a consequence of the implacable law of unified market that Marx laid bare in the above-quoted passage. The bourgeoisie succeeded in 'remaking the world in its own image' through ideological means, through the prestige of the dominant society and its model of 'good living', spread far and wide by the mass media. On the five continents, people drink Coca-Cola, eat the same brand of jam, listen to the same television programme promoting the same gadgets, and live huddled in beehives of the same monotonous concrete.

▪ The long-distance migrations of millions of people, supposedly characteristic of a distant prehistory and definitively relegated to the past by the 'progress' of our sedentary societies, have resumed on a global scale. The poverty-stricken surplus white work-force of the industrialized or semi-industrialized countries of Europe has spread out in the direction of new centres of capitalist growth in North America and South America, South Africa and Australia. Colonial manpower has been transported overseas *en masse* to meet the needs of the plantations, mines and ports of America, Africa and Oceania. Blacks in the eighteenth century, Chinese and Indians in the nineteenth and twentieth, have scattered all over the earth. And these movements have recently been supplemented by the importation of labour from the Third World and the semi-developed countries by the main industrial centres. Turks and Yugoslavs go to Germany; West Indians, Pakistanis and Africans to England: Mediterraneans and Africans to France. A process that in the nineteenth century was necessary only to the periphery of capitalism, where the colonial plantation economy imported its workers, has now become a necessity at the heart of the system.

▪ The global character of capitalist society is also expressed by the development of world systems of political domination and by the operation of historic influences of international scope – e.g., world wars and world crises. When the Emperor Charles V proudly declared that the sun would never set on the Hispano–Austrian Empire, he was expressing a historical *necessity* much more fundamental than the dynastic triumphs and colonial conquests of the Habsburgs in the sixteenth century. The great modern colonial empires, mainly the British and the French, were characterized by the same universality, and more recently we have witnessed the international ventures of the dollar and the C.I.A. Since the nineteenth century, economic crises – market gluts, overproduction, wild speculation, collapsing prices, unemployment – have been able to create chain reactions affecting the industrial and agricultural prosperity of widely separated areas. The collapse of the speculative bull market of Wall Street in 1929 brought ruin to entire agricultural districts of Burma, caused Brazilian coffee to be used in locomotive furnaces, upset the delicate economic balance of the Pacific islands that depend exclusively on the exportation of copra, threw the frenzied petty bourgeoisie of Germany into the arms of Hitler, prepared the way for the Popular Front in France and the Civil War in Spain. The world wars of the twentieth century directly or indirectly affected the entire planet through the wide dispersion of the various theatres of land and sea operations, the mobilization and movements of the military labour-force (the 'armies') and civilian personnel, the complete reorientation of industrial production, the crisis of political power in the colonial and semi-colonial countries, foreign occupations, etc. International society has organized as never before politically and administratively, acquiring special structures superimposed on supposedly sovereign states – the League of Nations after the First World War, for example, then the United Nations after the Second, not to mention a confusing alphabet-soup of technical agencies that increasingly supervise every aspect of social life, including air traffic control, Interpol, medical regulations, etc.

■ The modern revolutionary political forces also operate on a world scale. This was true for the revolutionary democratic pro-Jacobin ideals that found an echo as far from France as Chile and Egypt, New England and Batavia, Russia and Mysore, already in the early years of the nineteenth century. It is still truer of the revolutionary anti-capitalist movements. The three workers' 'Internationals', the ideology of socialism, Marxism, and finally Western leftism have been, and still are, political forces of universal scope.

But all these tendencies towards the global unification of world history encounter limitations imposed by the very mechanisms of the capitalist economy, and we are concerned here with one of its basic contradictions. On the one hand, capitalism unifies and levels all the peoples of the world, enveloping them in the same law of profits and productivity. But this same capitalism also deepens the gap between the privileged minorities and the mass of the world's peoples whom it exploits and *must* exploit. This phenomenon of polarization is already a fact of life within the developed capitalist societies. But it also operates on the international plane between the 'rich countries' and the 'poor countries'. Since the time when the latter achieved their formal political independence following the Second World War, the gap between the two categories has widened. The fact that the privileged élites of the West fiercely exploit the workers and the small employees of their own countries and live comfortably at their expense in no way alters the reality of the contrast and opposition between the rich and poor countries. Every inhabitant of an industrialized country, even if he is exploited at home, benefits from the *overall* situation of the society to which he belongs, in comparison with the poorer countries, and this is true regardless of the existence, in the poor countries, of profiteers and exploiters who are in collusion with the privileged elements of the rich countries. If, for example, the labour force of the poor countries were remunerated at the same rate as that of the rich countries – in terms of legal minimum wages, paid vacations, social security, etc. – the prices of the overwhelming majority of goods imported from the Third World would immediately skyrocket to prohibitive levels.

The supermarkets would be deserted, for the mass of ordinary customers who regularly pack them benefit willy nilly — and despite being themselves exploited — from the fact that the workers of the poor countries are much more exploited than they are. It has been estimated that the United States, with only 6 per cent of the world's population, gobbles up approximately 43 per cent of the world's resources. This means that the living standards reached by this small minority of people — despite the presence among them of both exploiters and exploited — is necessarily based on the poverty of the rest of the world. It can be shown by a simple mathematical calculation that if 6 per cent more people were to attain the living standards now enjoyed by the United States, they would consume another 43 per cent of the globe's resources. Only the remainder — in other words: $100 - (2 \times 43) = 14$ per cent — would be available for the other 88 per cent of the human race. A rough calculation, perhaps, but one that goes to the heart of the hypocrisy that is hidden behind words like 'underdeveloped countries' or 'developing countries'. Such terms are only the ideological rationalization of the enormous gap resulting from a fierce competition between peoples equipped with vastly unequal means at the outset. But no 'laggard' from the 'underdeveloped' countries will ever succeed in catching up without going over to the side of the exploiters — and the seats there are rare and dear. It is not a question of a simple mechanical discrepancy between mutually autonomous groups all starting out from a relatively favourable initial position. The exploitation is structural; there is a cause-and-effect relationship between the poverty of some and the prosperity of others.

In the grip of his all-encompassing vision of the levelling effects of capitalism and their tremendous consequences ('The bourgeoisie . . . draws all, even the most barbarous nations, into civilization'), Marx was less aware of the reverse tendency — the polarization between exploiting and exploited countries — although he did produce some cogent pages on the indispensable contribution of Indian poverty to England's economic take-off in the eighteenth century. Today, it is precisely this polarization effect that impresses us. The world city, as they say in China, can continue, in its present form and at its present level, only at the expense of the world village, only by exploiting it with increasing intensity.

12 National 'belongingness' in history

The nation-state-market as the historical field of the bourgeoisie – the urge for national identity in history – the reconquest of their national identities by the peoples of the Third World – the crisis of the Western nation-states and the movement of what are described, for want of a better term, as 'national minorities' – national 'belongingness' and participation in world-wide processes – 'The Chinese revolution is part of the world revolution' – the new internationalism has not yet found itself

The unifying role of capitalism is limited by still another contradiction: it has stimulated the polarization of international society into nations that are better structured than the empires, tribes or peoples of past ages.

Nations in the full sense of the term made their appearance in the West during the eighteenth and nineteenth centuries as capitalist relations solidified. They were homogeneous units, historical communities cemented economically by the unified national market and politically by the national state. Such *nation-state-markets* constituted the historical field required by the rising bourgeoisie in France, Germany and Great Britain, as well as in other countries of Europe. On the basis of even an incomplete community of language, culture, historical traditions, collective psychology, the bourgeoisie can bring together the political and territorial structures, the human resources it needs to achieve its economic plans and ambitions – the expanded reproduction of capital.

The international society of the nineteenth century was organized on the basis of these nation-state-markets and all they implied: the sovereignty of each state, the development of diplomatic relations and international law, the appearance, in embryo, of the first supranational institutions. When other peoples achieved their independence following the gradual break-up of the Spanish, German, Turkish, French, British, Italian and Portuguese empires, the nation-state-market still served as their structural model. These peoples found it necessary to follow the national pattern and to adapt to the structures of international society as they had been set up to the advantage of the Western bourgeoisie.

Their promotion to the status of national state was regarded as a political victory and temporarily masked the negative consequences, the heavy social and economic cost, entailed by their alignment with the capitalist West. From this point of view, these 'liberated' peoples remained, and still remain, imprisoned in the nation-state, the bourgeoisie's historical field of operation. This is true even for Vietnam, even for Cuba, even for China. And the peoples of the Third World who are still struggling for national liberation – Bangladesh and Biafra in the recent past, perhaps Eritrea or the Kurds in the near future – seem fated to try, in their turn, to fit into the familar mould of the nation-state.

As Zhou En-lai expressed it in 1970 on receiving a delegation of American academics from the Committee of Concerned Asian Scholars: 'We are living in a world of nations.' A realistic observation, and one that was anything but enthusiastic – far removed, in any case, from the visionary analyses of Marx, who waxed lyrical over the unifying capacities of capitalism: 'In place of the old local seclusion and self-sufficiency, we have intercourse in every direction, universal interdependence of nations.' The interdependence is a reality – and is accompanied, at least superficially, by an increasing polarization around the nation-states.

What does all this imply for historical knowledge, for our relationship to the past? At the nation-state level, each people strives to impose its presence on the international stage by asserting its national identity as a long-standing historical fact. Each tries – we have encountered this problem in connection with the abuses of quadripartism – to order its past in terms of the decisive watersheds of its own history. For the Greeks, the emphasis is on the fall of Byzantium and the end of the Turkish occupation. For Vietnam, the key dates are the coming of the French in 1858 and the August Revolution of 1945 that proclaimed the inauguration of the Democratic Republic. For China, the main historical events are the Opium War and the 4 May movement.

The urge for *national belongingness* is particularly marked among the peoples who have been incorporated for centuries into large politico-historical units that were successively made and unmade by military conquest or dynastic upheavals. An example is Egypt, nucleus of the ancient empires of the Pharaohs, later a province in turn of the Persian, Alexandrian, Roman, Byzantine, Arab, Ottoman and British empires. Egypt was integrated into each of these imperial structures of widely varying scope and nature. Yet Egypt possesses a long-standing historical continuity of its own, over and above the discontinuity of the empires to which it has belonged; and it has a sharp awareness of this continuity. The same is true of Belgium. It was successively an integral part of Roman Gaul, of the empire of Charlemagne, of the Germanic Holy

Roman Empire, of the Burgundian states at the end of the Middle Ages, of the Habsburg empire, of revolutionary and Napoleonic France, of the Kingdom of the Netherlands; and it was only after 1830 that Belgium acquired a distinct personality of its own, which is now shaken once again by the struggle between rival linguistic groups. Yet Belgian history reaches back a long way. The Belgian country of today was part of that distinct Belgian history at each stage of its development, regardless of the larger political entities in which it was successively included.

National continuity and national identity can be taken for granted in the case of countries like Germany or France. But in the case of the great majority of peoples, especially those in nearly all the Third World countries, they imply a struggle, a reconquest transcending what is euphemistically called the 'colonial interlude' — in other words, the period during which those countries were integrated by force into the 'sphere of influence' of the industrialized West. In the contemporary Philippines, for example, there is considerable emphasis on the people's pre-Hispanic 'national roots', on everything that tends to link the independent Philippines of today with the Malaysian tribes of five centuries ago. In Vietnam, the reconquest of national continuity takes place at the level of language itself and the political concepts it conveys. Throughout the entire period of French domination, the word Vietnam had disappeared and with it the idea that a Vietnamese national reality existed. The talk was of 'Indochina', of 'Indochinese' history, which amounted to a double denial of the Vietnamese nation. It was assimilated to Laos and Cambodia, countries with completely different historical backgrounds, and at the same time it was split up into entities without the slightest political or historical substance, such as Tonkin, Annam, Cochin-China. In both cases, the structures of French imperialism were imposed from outside. All the official references were to 'Indochinese' history, with its succession of Governor-Generals, its economic expansion, its colonial police regime, its progress toward 'civilization'. To reintegrate the eighty years of 'Indochinese' history under French domination means restoring to those years their national substance. The Vietnamese historians continue, of course, to take into account the impact of colonial domination during the 'Indochinese' era; it is, after all, a fact. But they particularly emphasize Vietnamese reactions to that domination and the stages in the development of the Vietnamese national movement — the stage of leadership by the old Confucian scholars; the stage of fruitless efforts by the Vietnamese bourgeoisie to impose its leadership; finally, the stage of working-class leadership following the foundation of the Indochinese Communist Party in 1930.

The reconquest of internal historical continuity often means the 'revival' of a whole series of historical achievements that were deliberately eclipsed during the period when the peoples in question lived under the domination of the West. This is the significance of the return of the 'boubous' – those loose, colourful African robes – as official dress in Black Africa, or the systematic revival, in China or Vietnam, of traditional medical knowledge such as acupuncture or moxibustion, a process of cauterization by the application of a substance that is burned slowly on the skin. All this ancient lore was forced into a kind of hibernation during the long period when only the practice of Western medicine could be a source of prestige and profit in the Far East. In Vietnam, this revival policy is called 'the development of ancient capital'.

It is therefore the responsibility of each people to assess their own past, to identify both the negative elements and those that can serve as an encouragement to their present hopes and struggles. In 1940, Mao called for a critical summing-up of Chinese history:

> During the thousands of years of recorded history, the Chinese nation has given birth to many national heroes and revolutionary leaders. Thus, the Chinese nation has a glorious revolutionary tradition and a splendid historical heritage. . . .
>   Our national history goes back several thousand years and has its own characteristics and innumerable treasures. But in these matters we are mere schoolboys. Contemporary China has grown out of the China of the past; we are Marxist in our historical approach and must not lop off our history. We should sum up our history from Confucius to Sun Yat-sen and take over this valuable legacy. (*Selected Works of Mao Tse-Tung*, Volume II.)

The emphasis on national history does not mean that there is nothing to be learned from the historical experience of other peoples. But a certain preference for the national is inescapable, as is demonstrated, for example, by the importance of folklore passed on in early childhood from generation to generation, the implicit message of proverbs and street-names, customary affinities, the unspoken content of social experience. Everyone is more comfortable with his own people's past. But this national emphasis is fruitless unless expressed in class terms and only historians with roots among the people can lay claim to it. A member of the *Andrina* aristocracy in Madagascar cannot, for example, face up to the fact that, before the French conquest, the entire history of Madagascar was based on the antagonism between slaves and kings. His historical rhetoric is little more than a substitute for that of the despised *Vazaha* (white) historians. In history, the emphasis on the national is a privilege of the masses.

But today the nation-states, at least in the capitalist West, are being shaken from within. Far from being 'completed' once and for all and far from controlling the historical future, they are challenged by vigorous anti-centralist movements. These movements reject the prevailing discrimi-

nations against the older inhabitants of their regions or against the new-
comers – like the Indians, Blacks or Chicanos in the United States, or the
immigrant workers in Western Europe – who are drawn to the area as
cheap labour by the mechanism of the labour market. The new movements
refuse to accept the traditional regional handicaps or the economic, cultural or linguistic oppression of minority peoples in the interest of the
ruling classes or the dominant ethnic groups. This is true of the Scots,
the Welsh and the Irish of the 'United Kingdom', the Catalans, Galicians
and Basques of Spain, the Walloons of Belgium, the Sicilians, Sardinians
and Tyroleans of Italy. In France, a country proudly described as the
most perfect expression of a long historical process of nation-building,
the anti-centralist struggles of the Corsicans and Catalans, the Basques
and the Alsatians, the Occitans and the Bretons, have demonstrated the
scope and intensity of the crisis in the very heart of the developed capitalist nation-states.

The theoretical analysis of all these movements is only beginning and
it is probably impossible to define them in terms of a single model. However they are analyzed, they can certainly not be interpreted as a 'third
wave' of nationalist movements succeeding the national struggles of the
nineteenth century in Europe and the Third World liberation movements
of the twentieth. They are expressions of the crisis of developed capitalist
society and are striking at its heart, not its periphery. They are challenging
both the classical nation-state and the new multinational imperialism.
They are putting forward political demands that the nation-states cannot
satisfy, either in the case of landless minorities (like the oppressed ethnic
groups of the USA or the immigrant workers of Western Europe) or in the
case of minorities living in territories of their own in Europe. These movements raise in a new way the old problem of the transition to socialism
in the developed capitalist societies.

The crisis of the nation-states is already playing havoc with the prevailing historical rhetoric. The minority peoples are reclaiming their own
past and striving – as in France and the United States – to reconquer it.
Many examples of their struggle have been mentioned in this book. They
resist oppression by appealing to their past and thereby force us to re-
consider the entire historical process that gave rise to the modern French
and American nations. The anti-centralist struggles of contemporary
France force us to confront what the building of the 'French nation' cost
the various peoples who constitute it today. The cost can be calculated,
for example, in terms of the demographic blood-drain required for France's
wars, and of the displacement of people in the construction of a bureaucratic state apparatus or in the industrial development of the North and
the East. It can also be assessed in terms of forced cultural assimilation
through the primary school or military service, or in terms of distorted

economic development, the negation of political originality or the denial
of the right to be 'different'. French centralist history traditionally treats
all these phenomena as regrettable but minor 'slips', of small importance
alongside the slow, majestic construction of the nation-state by the kings
and the bourgeois republics from Richelieu and Colbert to Napoleon, from
the Jacobins to De Gaulle.

The struggles of each people are mainly an aspect of their own internal
development. But they are also an aspect of the *international* historical
process. Historical analysis must bring out both these aspects, always show
ing that they are inextricably linked and not mere separate 'factors' that
can be cautiously added to the stew of scholarship: a drop of internation
ism, plus a pinch of national character.

▪ The foundation of the Chinese Communist party in 1921 was the fruit
of both an internal maturation process – the 4th of May events, the
development of the Chinese national movement towards Marxism and the
proletariat – and an outside intervention, symbolized by the arrival of
the Moscow delegates in China to carry out the Comintern's new line of
temporarily bypassing Europe in order to concentrate on Asia. Today,
the Soviet position papers emphasize the second aspect, while the Chinese
emphasize the first. But neither the internal maturation nor the outside
intervention would have been possible without the other.

▪ May '68 derived its force from the merging of the internal crisis of
Gaullism, as expressed by a gigantic strike wave ('Ten years is enough!'
shouted the demonstrating workers), with a worldwide upsurge of youth
and student struggles. But the unity of these two aspects was never fully
attained; it remained a mere possibility. As a result, May '68 floundered.

▪ In May 1970, 100,000 people marched in protest against the Vietnam
war in the streets of Melbourne: the most powerful political demonstration since the arrival of Captain Cook. The appeal of the broad-based
Vietnam Moratorium Committee that sponsored the demonstration acted
as a catalyst for a whole series of domestic discontents in Australia: wide
spread weariness after twenty years of conservative rule, inflation, politic
and economic stagnation.

The problem of the relationship between national identification and
worldwide repercussions or influences raises the related question of
internationalism, its necessity and limits. What is really meant by the
frequently-quoted statement: 'The Chinese Revolution is part of the
World Revolution'? This statement constitutes, of course, an appeal for
moral support, for solidarity. It proclaims that every revolutionary movement needs the help of other peoples, but that its very success produces,
at the same time, a chain reaction that facilitates the armed struggle of
other peoples. The Vietnam war exerted a catalytic, unifying effect on
all the struggles of the American Left, including those of feminists, Black

Chicanos, counter-culturists, students, war-resisters, etc. At the same time, all these movements contributed inside the United States to the progressive weakening and isolation of the American power-structure and its war policy.

International solidarity implies organized contacts and exchanges of experience, for it is based on common objectives: it is the struggle of all the world's peoples against the world capitalist system. And yet capitalism is so highly integrated a system that the fight against it is indivisible, and no particular area, branch of activity or country can feel it has triumphed so long as the system as a whole remains under the control of the enemy. When the Chinese say that their Revolution is part of the World Revolution, they also mean that it partakes of the delays, limits, setbacks of the latter. It is a much less optimistic and idealistic statement than many seem to think. Internationalism encounters the weight of realities, this ever-present 'world of nations'. The great danger facing the people's revolutions of our time is that of getting bogged down in the worldwide rivalry of the nation-states, the so-called 'concert of nations'. The Soviet Union of Lenin's time intended originally to have a much more open political structure, free of specific national characteristics. But reality and the hard fact of Russian nationalism, in a situation of capitalist encirclement, got the upper hand.

One of the main contradictions of our time (and here we return to the problem of national 'belongingness' in history) is that, although we are living in a highly integrated world of standardized technique where multinational companies and international organs of repression like Interpol are all-powerful and information flows from continent to continent, the fact remains that the mass of people are able to act only within the framework of their own national state, large or small. The key aspect of this contradiction is what the Chinese Marxists call 'the priority of internal factors'. To take the example of Vietnam again, it must be recognized that the powerful movement of international solidarity with the victims of the American escalation between 1965 and 1970 was never really an integral part of the mass struggles around domestic issues that always took priority. With the possible exception of the United States, the people of the West remained 'Far from Vietnam' — to borrow the title of a striking documentary film about the international Vietnam solidarity movement produced by a group of French cineasts in those years.

Similarly, the worldwide emotion aroused by the tragic death of the Marxist premier of Chile, Salvador Allende, and the butchery that followed it soon faded, for it was not linked to the ongoing people's struggles in the various countries. Yet the world forces that crushed the Chilean people are the same as those that combat the movement in every country: the multinational companies and capitalist exploitation, the military bureaucracy, male chauvinism, etc. But the connection was not made explicit because the adversary wears a different mask in each country and acts through a series of different intermediaries. In February 1962, following the massacre perpetrated by the police at a Métro station during an anti-colonialist demonstration in a working-class district of Paris, a million people spontaneously came out on the streets. Yet the death sentences pronounced, and executed, by the Franco regime in Spain did not arouse the same concern in France. The mass of the people react in a qualitatively different way to 'external' and 'internal' problems; foreign affairs remain quite 'foreign'.

National 'belongingness' and international interdependence are linked only potentially. The new internationalism has yet to find itself.

13 Merging natural history and social history

Nature is part of our historical field of action — there can be no 'history without people' — the ecology debacle reflects a basic contradiction of capitalism: the discrepancy between its urge for unlimited self-expansion and limited natural resources — socialism must prove itself by its ability to control the 'impetuous progress' of the productive forces — the ecology struggle invades the political area; it enters history

The point is to bring natural history into social history and not, as some are tempted to do, to drag man back into a state of nature, in a reaction against the recent perversions of uncontrolled growth and the entire complex social machinery. Such an approach is currently fashionable: let man return to the 'simple life' and resume his place in the natural cycle. Its final aim is to reduce man to his zoological dimension in a 'society' of a minimal technological level comparable to that of bees or beavers.

Bringing natural history into social history is an entirely different matter. It amounts to an affirmation of the power, and therefore the responsibility, of man with respect to the entire natural world.

It is not a question of setting up a mechanical opposition between man and nature. 'Wild' nature, as the French ethnographer S. Moscovici has pointed out, is also very largely shaped by man. Nature is no less a part of history than are man and society (see *La Société contre nature*). The so-called 'wild' species, for example, are precisely those that man has spared because he lacked either the time or the desire to destroy them. The 'natural' ecological complexes — the savannas, the forests, the steppes — are nearly always the product of a complicated web of relationships among plants, animals and *man* in his role (even if only intermittent) as woodcutter, shepherd, farmer, etc.

As Engels put it in *The Dialectics of Nature*: 'we by no means rule over nature like a conqueror over a foreign people, like someone standing outside nature — but . . . we, with flesh, blood and brain, belong to nature.'

For this reason, it is extremely naïve to suppose — as do some would-be historical 'innovators' — that there can be such a thing as a 'history without people', a history of the natural world in time. To apply the label 'historical' to all the varieties of long-range time — astronomical time, geological time, evolutionary biological time — may serve to flatter the professional pride of the historians, but its usefulness stops there. If what is meant, on the other hand, is the study of natural phenomena in the human time-scale, then the so-called 'history without people' is a contradiction in terms. To study climatic changes, volcanos or coastal formations over a relatively brief time-span, some thousands of years, is meaningless except in relationship to man in the role of witness, analyst or supporting agent of such phenomena. They are of significance for the historian only to the extent that man takes their measure, integrates them into his own sphere of activity. Marc Bloch made this point with reference to the silting up of the Zuyder Zee, which was a neutral, purely 'geological', phenomenon in appearance only:

> In the tenth century, a deep bay, the Zwin, indented the Flemish coast. Then it silted up. To which discipline or branch of knowledge does the study of this phenomenon belong? Geology comes first to mind. The shifting of alluvial deposits, the role of marine currents, perhaps changes in the ocean levels — was not geology invented to deal with precisely such matters? Certainly. But on taking a closer look, it is not so simple.
>
> First of all, the origins of the change have to be examined! And already our geologist finds himself confronted with questions that go beyond his field. For the clogging of the bay was undoubtedly facilitated by the construction of dams, the deflection of the sewers, drainage — all acts of human beings, dictated by social needs and conceivable only in the framework of a particular social structure.
>
> At the other end, a new problem arises — what of the consequences? Not far from the bay, a city was built. It was called Bruges, and was linked to the bay by a short expanse of river; through the waters of the Zwin, it could receive or ship off merchandise and so became, in a sense, the London or New York of its day. Then followed the gradual filling in of the bay. As the flooded surface receded, the docks of Bruges progressively ceased to function, despite all efforts to move the outer ports further and further towards the river's mouth. This was not, of course, the only cause of the city's eclipse — far from it! Does the physical process ever act upon the social unless its impact has been facilitated by other factors — human factors? But in the complex web of causation, that particular cause was undoubtedly among the most decisive. (*Apologie pour l'histoire.*)

We instinctively realize that the way a given society reshapes the very land on which it thrives is a distinctly 'historical' fact.

It is from this perspective that we must examine the ecological crisis — the environment crisis — that has become so acute today. It is a crisis caused by so-called 'wild' technological growth, but it derives from the

sential mechanisms of the capitalist system and its basic economic
w — the pursuit of profit.

In Marx's day, nature may well have appeared as an unlimited reserve
industrial, alimentary and energy resources. It was seen as a field of
tivity for human production — the basis of the 'productive forces'
hose never-ending development was for Marx, that optimistic child of
e Enlightenment, the central thread of human history. The only
oblem was to subjugate nature.

Capitalism today is entering a qualitatively new phase characterized
/ the discrepancy between the *limitless* demands of capital growth, of
s constantly expanding reproduction, on the one hand, and, on the
her, the *limited* resources provided by nature. This contradiction is
w. Marx and Engels were not in a position to analyze it for, in their
me, the phenomena of the destruction of the environment were embry-
ic, localized — they did not yet constitute the principal aspect of the
velopment of industrial capitalism. And this, by the way, emphasizes
th the fruitfulness and the limitations of Marxist principles, the neces-
ty of applying them in a creative way. The dogmatists are intellectually
comfortable with the environment and growth crises, for there are no
arxist quotations to serve as guideposts to mark out this unfamiliar
rrain. They fall back on the statement that such problems will auto-
atically disappear with the disappearance of capitalism. The modernists,
r their part, claim that Marx is 'outdated'. Yet this contradiction
tween unlimited capitalist self-expansion and the limited resources of
iture cannot possibly be analyzed effectively without reference to
arxism. But this is an analysis that Marx himself did not — and could
t — carry out.

Man has always, of course, been an active transformer of nature. He
is modified the vegetable balance (by his pastures, for example), the
imate (by the irrigation of crops in desert areas), the coast and river
drography (by dikes, canals and dams), the surface of the earth (by
rraces on the slopes). But the basis cycles of the natural world were
t affected by all these activities. Today a critical threshold has been
ached, for the basic cycles have now been affected in a fundamental
d perhaps irreversible way.

The climatological balance is threatened by nuclear explosions in the
pper atmosphere, by supersonic planes, by the slow formation of an
ivelope of carbonic gas around the earth. This envelope may eventually
terfere with the heat exchanges between earth and space, resulting in
catastrophic heating of the entire atmosphere — what is called the
reenhouse effect.

The hydrographic and bio-hydrographic balance is threatened by
emical pollution, sewers, detergents, thermal pollution caused by

factories using refrigeration techniques, and by nuclear power stations. The Mediterranean and the Baltic have become virtually dead seas. The American Great Lakes, those inexhaustible fishing reserves in the days of Fenimore Cooper, have been transformed into huge sewers.

■ The biological balance is threatened by the accumulation of non-biodegradable material on land and sea. It is also threatened by a series of chemical products accumulated in the bodies of animals, vegetables and men. In Brittany, the policy of the 1960s of stimulating agricultural productivity resulted in grouping together the scattered lots of the peasants with the aim of shortening their travel time back and forth from work and enabling them to make use of farming equipment on a large scale. This reorganization (*remembrement*) process destroyed the hedges and made the micro-climate less tolerable by amplifying the effect of cold weather, of draught and heat; it also interfered with the channelling of running water and led to the death of birds that feed on insects.

Bringing natural history into social history means taking the measure of man's responsibility towards nature and himself — not out of a mystical feeling for nature, but because of the importance of the stakes involved.

The main culprit is the profit system. From the viewpoint of vulgar, dogmatic Marxism, the 'irrepressible advance' of productive forces is the mainspring of social progress. As the contradiction between the development of productive forces and the stagnation of relations of production under capitalism intensifies, socialism comes closer to reality. But this outlook leads to a kind of 'fetichism of productive forces', which in the last analysis amounts to little more than a new ideological twist to the basic philosophy of capitalism: the glorification of productivity and growth as the supreme value. This version of socialism preserves, and projects into the future, all the basic characteristics of capitalism — a system that requires unlimited growth as a condition of its continued existence. But this unlimited growth comes inevitably into contradiction with nature's limited resources.

What all this means is that the question of the relationship between swiftly developing productive forces and a stagnating social order must be raised in a new way. In order to bring to an end the environmental mess and the negative effects of productivist growth with a view to endless profit-making, the growth of productive forces must be controlled *selectively* in terms of social needs. But selective control does not imply a policy of 'zero growth' as suggested by certain technocrats who use this slogan to hide blatant social inequalities inside the Western world and between the peoples of the northern and southern hemispheres. Such growth control makes the traditional relationship between the productive forces and productive relations more complex. Social consciousness exerts an increasing influence on the course of history.

The environmental crisis demands, then, a better definition of socialism, which can now be viewed as the social order capable of controlling, in the most effective and responsible way, its relationship with nature and the expansion of its productive forces. It is also the social order capable of liberating those productive forces from the tyranny of profits and productivity and from the fetichism of growth as an end in itself. This gives us a useful criterion for judging the socialist character of the Soviet Union, the People's Democracies of Europe, or of People's China. Bohemia, the industrial stronghold of the Soviet bloc, shamelessly empties the waste-matter of its factories into the Vltava, the Elbe, and the North Sea. And when, in 1975, the left-wing ideologists of the Shanghai group declared that China was still living under the reign of 'bourgeois law', and that the imperatives of a capitalist society had not yet been completely eliminated, they were acknowledging the existence of numerous unsolved problems — for example, the thick blanket of smoke over the big cities, the widespread misuse of poisonous pesticides in the country villages, the ruining of the water supply in industrial areas.

Today, the reciprocal man-nature relationship has moved to the forefront of human history. Not only have numerous cries of alarm been sounded in France and particularly in the United States by people like Rachel Carson, Barry Commoner and many others, but the ecology issue has now directly invaded the arena of traditional politics. The campaign against nuclear power stations, though boycotted by 'responsible' political groups of the Left as well as of the Right, has won as much mass support in France as in Sweden, West Germany and the English-speaking countries. And a militant struggle over a supposedly 'secondary' issue like sea pollution has given tremendous impetus to an awakening political consciousness in Corsica. The campaign of the agronomist René Dumont during the 1974 French Presidential election was another example of how the ecology issue is breaking into traditional politics. Dismissed as 'utopian' at first, that campaign finally aroused far more interest than the substantial score of 300,000 votes for the candidate of 'political ecology' would seem to indicate.

For the political struggle of consistent ecologists — unlike the defenders of summer bungalows or obsolete professional privileges — constitutes a direct challenge to the capitalist system. In that respect — and here we return to the idea of bringing natural history into social history — it is profoundly *historical,* since it is based on a sharp awareness of the impact of human action throughout time. This is certainly true of the 'short run'. The ecologists are always reminding us, for example, that, according to official statistics, an entire French Departement is gobbled up by concrete every five years — in other words, an area equivalent to one of the ninety administrative units into which the country is divided is ruthlessly overrun in that period of time by new highways, supermarkets, parking-lots, filling-stations, housing projects, newfangled gimmicky residential complexes. And this process of reckless super-urbanization has already been under way for some time.

The new ecological awakening also takes the long-run time-span into account. The ecologists' indictment of the capitalist system is solidly rooted in an active, militant relationship to the past. It is a relationship that is constantly fed by the memories of older people who recall, for example, the time when the bread had some taste and there were fish in the river! It is enriched by all the traditional know-how — cooking recipes, home-made medicines, etc. — these older people can pass on to help us escape the technological tyranny of contemporary society and become aware of the falseness of many current needs.

This sense of time is also oriented toward the future, 'What kind of planet will we bequeath to our children?' The very question is an affirmation of mankind's historical dimension as contrasted with the historical 'weightlessness' of capitalist society and its glorification of a rootless, airtight present.

The ecological crisis which has so deeply shaken the West has been perceived quite differently in the Third World. This is the reflection of another of capitalism's basic contradictions: the so-called 'developed' countries and the dependent ones are poles apart in every respect. The ecological mess is not as yet the preoccupation of a Third World still crushed under the weight of famine and poverty. The administrators and leaders of the newly created states — even the most honest and disinterested among them — are in no position to assess the long-term negative effects of uncontrolled environment-destroying industrial development against its obvious short-term benefits: increased productivity, new jobs, etc. The 'poor' side of the Mediterranean, its southern bank, is even more intensely polluted than the 'rich' side by the waste-matter of industry, of the big cities and the oil tankers. And within the framework of capitalism there exists no overall solution to the global problem of ecological disaster. Once again, the peoples who exploit others cannot themselves be free, cannot become the collective masters of their relationship to the natural world.

4 The short run and the long run: continuity and discontinuity in history

*e long-run approach: 'massive' history or passive history? – dialectical
ity in the 'short run' and the 'long run': moments, wars, elections –
erdetermined contradictions in history – the concept of 'generation'
historical flux, Soviet-style and Chinese-style – intellectual contro-
rsies about the plurality of long-range periods and political thoughts
t the active use of historical roots.*

e 'long-run' approach is fashionable among historians. For nearly half
century now, a certain school of French historians, following in the
otsteps of Lucien Febvre and Marc Bloch, founders of the *Annales,*
ve been taking great pains to present it as an innovation. They sneer
the 'history of battles' and consider it the ultimate dishonour to
scend to the level of 'event-centred' history. In their eyes, what counts
the 'basic fabric of history', the history of trade-routes or of popular
titudes, changes in the demographic balance, in handicraft techniques,
eating habits or in the mechanisms of sickness and death throughout
e centuries. Imagination is not lacking among these 'pioneers of
storical knowledge', these 'pathfinders' – to use the triumphant
cabulary of Pierre Nora and Jacques Le Goff in *Faire de l'histoire,* a
cent work giving ample scope to these 'new fields'.
 Moreover, since the advent of structuralism in the social sciences
wards the end of the 1950s, the 'long-run' approach seems to have
fered historians an effective and attractive way out of a dilemma.
ey could not avoid taking into consideration the development of
cial experience throughout historical time, the 'diachrony'; but at the
me time, they had to meet the new demands of the structural
proach. So the more they overlooked the ephemeral upheavals – wars,
volutions, 'situations' – that supposedly shook only the surface of
story, the more they could plunge into a so-called 'deeper' reality
hose relative stability apparently put historians on the same level as
ructuralists in social science.
 But what kind of historical 'long run' interests them? It is one that
kes the masses of people into account only as human beings who,

individually or in groups, consumed, worked, invented techniques and then either transmitted or forgot them, reproduced, fell sick, developed folk culture – in other words, *accepted* their fate. This 'massive' history is in reality a passive history. The 'long run' so dear to the hearts of the new historians is a depoliticized 'long run'. To confirm this we have only to glance at the table of contents of *Faire de l'histoire*, the bound volumes of the *Annales,* or the titles of the articles the leading lights of this particular school regularly contribute to the *Nouvel Observateur,* their special forum. Such things as wars, international power systems, political power struggles, revolutions, hardly interest them at all. Or if they do, it is only to drain them of significance as was done with the French Revolution which, it seems, was neither a bourgeois nor a popular revolution, but a mere outburst of angry crowds or the skilful displacement of a few political leaders. In fact, the entire political dimension is missing in these long-run phenomena in which the modernists specialize. They collect mountains of data, for example, about eating habits in the seventeenth century but ignore the critical question of who ate well, who ate inadequately and *why* – the role of hunger and satiety in the political relationship of forces and the class-struggle.

The 'long run' is certainly a reality – a reality no less political than the facts described in the much-deprecated event-centred history. *The genuine political field, yesterday as today, consists precisely in the unity of the long run and the short run.*

But what kind of politics is meant? Certainly not the politics of the diplomatic or official accounts produced by the traditional pre-1914 historians. In the last analysis, politics is an affair of the masses of people. And for them the only meaning that exists is a political one. Culture and technique, sickness and food – all take on significance only to the extent that they brake or stimulate mass struggles. At the same time, no political change is genuine unless it affects every aspect of the individual's personal life, unless it touches the family, our relationship to nature, our attitudes towards work tools, towards death itself. As Gramsci expressed it, changes in the 'political' society are merely formal and superficial unless the 'civil' society also changes.

There are, of course, 'historical periods on a slope so slight as to be imperceptible to the naked eye,' wrote Michel Foucault in his *Archéologie du savoir.* But these too are an integral part of the political field. The French-German language border has not substantially changed in Lorraine since the Middle Ages: that is a political fact. Historical demography is a class demography; it brings out striking contrasts between the rich and the poor, and these contrasts have an undeniable impact on the class struggle. It is the task of the historian to define this impact. But such questions are never raised by the computer-minded historians.

Another example: Did the development of farming techniques during the Middle Ages reinforce the feudal order or did it, on the contrary, stimulate the rebellion of the peasantry, the *Jacquerie,* or the slow rise of the bourgeoisie? These questions cannot, of course, be answered unless someone is more interested in raising them than in collecting ancient engravings or old tools like the specialists in 'French ethnography' at the Museum of Popular Arts and Traditions in Paris.

The 'long run' is political – its continuity is only apparent, since it is punctuated by sharp breaks and violent upheavals. The inner essence of these mutations consists of both the 'long-run' phenomena and the sudden crisis that sets off the explosion. This is what is meant by the old saying: 'Happy people have no history.' For history, in the last analysis, consists essentially of upheavals and explosions – and the underlying developments that lead up to them. History is made up of 'revolutions', an expression that emphasizes political, economic and technological mutations. It is made up of 'moments', *momentum-movimentum*; the two words are complementary. Such 'moments' are both points in time and a complex of processes that have reached the breaking point. The scope and impact of such 'moments' therefore transcend the 'event', which is no more than its momentary expression. The argument over the merits of 'event-centred' history leads nowhere, for it concerns only the tip of the iceberg.

Take, for example, the 'moment' of 1789, which united in a single bundle of explosive contradictions the internal crisis of the ruling class, the crisis of the monarchy's state apparatus, especially in the financial sphere, the impetuous rise of the bourgeoisie in the sphere of production and trade, the short-term economic recession, the centuries-old impatience of the oppressed peasantry, the ideological crisis in which the philosophers played a key role.

Or the 'moment' of 1917–19, when the revolutionary movements of Europe reached maturity. The upheavals of the First World War and the widespread war-weariness of the peoples brought social contradictions to the boiling point in the major capitalist countries. This was true even among the victors: in France, there were the big strikes of 1919, while in Great Britain the Scottish workers were in a state of rebellion, and in northern Italy workers' councils were set up in the Piedmont region. In the defeated countries, the crisis was even sharper, with the upsurge of Sparticism in Germany and of revolutionary socialism in Vienna. But the weakest link was Russia where the Bolsheviks leapt into the breach. In all these countries – and not in Russia alone – the revolutionary explosion brought into play a whole series of social and cultural forces that had long been gathering force beneath the surface.

Or the 'moment' of May '68. The short-term crisis of Gaullism as an authoritarian political regime with a social policy of expansion at the expense of the working class triggered the outbreak of a deeper and more general social crisis that had been latent until them. May '68 raised the issue of the 'quality of life' in capitalist society and suddenly expanded the field of political action to include the struggles of immigrants of women, of regional minorities, of prisoners, of the counter-culture. Only those whose vision was limited to the 'events' of May '68 and the 'disorder' it created could say 'Never Again!', which became the slogan of both the classical Right and the classical Left in France.

1789! 1917–19! May '68! These three historical moments met three quite different fates: the successful rise of the bourgeoisie in the first case; in the second, the apparent victory of the Bolsheviks which was not accompanied by a more general European-wide revolution and therefore contained the seeds of future difficulties; in the third case, the short-term setback of the rebellion. But each of these moments is equally rich, equally loaded with significance. For unlike the ephemeral *event*, the historical *moment* raises the issue of the 'possible'; it is precisely in the 'moment' that 'everything is possible', as the rebels of May '68 expressed it, while reactionaries and moderates alike invariably stress the 'impossible'. For Ho Chi Minh, August 1945 – when the Vietnamese revolutionaries rose up and proclaimed the birth of an independent Republic – was the 'favourable moment' (*thoi co thuan loi*), a key concept of Vietnamese revolutionary strategy.

The dialectical linkage of the continuous and the discontinuous is the thread that runs throughout all history. The Chinese peasant movements, for example, derived their force from the slow, tireless action of the secret societies and other expressions of permanent but latent discontent in the countryside: draft resistance, tax and rent evasion, sporadic attacks against the rich and the exploiters. But the cumulative effect of all these separate struggles finally sparked off violent explosions in the form of massive uprisings and peasant wars of national scope such as those that threatened or, in some cases, even toppled the Han, Sui, Tang and Ming dynasties.

For 'wars' are not mere temporary phases of military violence alternating, like night and day, with phases of 'peace' and prosperity, though such is the mechanical and moralistic view of bourgeois history as it was of the monarchist history that preceded it. Wars are indeed 'the continuation of politics by other means', the expression of the same historical imperatives as those that operate in times of 'peace' – the quest for slave-labour under slavery, for possession of land (and the peasants who lived on it) under feudalism, for profits under capitalism.

Or take the 1914–18 war. The textbooks treat it as a merely military phenomenon. The classical approach is to distinguish the various phases

– first, the war of movement in the summer of 1914; then, a war of
position for four long years, with the trenches, the epic battle of Verdun,
the crumbling morale of the 'rear'; and finally the war of movement
again in 1918. Yet in reality, the war with its accompanying 'sacred
national union', did not, as is often asserted, temporarily suspend the
play of social and economic forces. For foreign war does not mean
'social peace'. On the contrary, the war of 1914–18 laid bare the basic
mechanics of French society under the Third Republic – the superficial
role of Parliament, the profitable business of war orders for the benefit
of shady industrialists, nationalist demagogy, the impotence of the
labour movement, the immorality of the ruling class's flaunted wealth
in the face of widespread poverty, famine and cold; the massive tapping
of the peasantry's financial and human resources (in gold and soldiers),
especially in the less industrialized areas like Brittany, Occitania, Corsica. For the basic understanding of a society, war is far richer than
'peace' – *far truer*. This applies to Nazi Germany, at war all over
Europe; to the United States, at war in Vietnam – and to France, at war
in Algeria.

The elections on which the politicians of both Right and Left single-
mindedly fix their attention are meaningless unless fitted into a relatively
long-range perspective. Even if we decide to discount the inevitable
fraud, jerry-mandering and ideological conditioning that accompany
them, elections at best only reflect, with a certain degree of accuracy, a
relationship of political forces that is determined *elsewhere*. The oft-
cited French elections of 1936, for example, spelled victory for the
Popular Front; but the legislature they brought into existence voted full
emergency powers to Pétain by an overwhelming majority in 1940. The
only real 'landslides' of contemporary French experience were those of
1945 and 1958 – the first gave a Parliamentary majority to the tripartite
arrangement (Communists, Socialists and the Catholic M.R.P.); the
second to De Gaulle and his followers. But a long period of preparation
in the mind of the population preceded and made possible the advent of
both the Fourth (1945) and the Fifth (1958) Republics, which in each
case merely confirmed a new political relationship of forces. The Fourth
Republic was the result of the Nazi Occupation, the Resistance, the
decomposition of the Third Republic. The Fifth was produced by the
impotence of the 'Third Force' parties and their sterile bickering, by
economic problems following the Liberation, by long and costly colonial
wars in Indochina and Algeria.

Louis Althusser has brilliantly analyzed the 'overdetermined contradictions' of history, stressing the interdependence of the specific
event and the underlying historical process, united in a coherent whole.
In analyzing the crisis of October 1917, he stresses the concrete situ-

ation in place and time with a clarity that contrasts sharply with the previous work of this writer, who has always opposed the concept of concrete history. Only superficially was October 1917 a marginal crisis, an exception to the basic contradictions of capitalism at the time. In Russia, the contradictions of capitalism may have seemed less ripe than elsewhere, but they became explosive through a combination of circumstances: a long war, an oppressed peasantry, economic underdevelopment, political despotism, the country's semicolonial status, the existence of a radical intelligentsia, etc. Russia was indeed the 'weakest link of the chain'.

How do the people cope with the dialectics of the long run and the short run? They sense that 'something is happening', that one era is giving way to another. Or else that nothing is really happening – that change is only apparent. For thousands of years, this sense of historical change was vague and confused, only half-real. But the awareness of living through a phase of historical change became increasingly acute over the years. In the period of the transition from feudalism to capitalism that awareness already assumed concrete historical and political shape, with the radicalism of Cromwell's time, the coming of the eighteenth-century enlightenment, the Jacobin Calendar of 1793. In the struggle for socialism, the conscious awareness of living through a change of era becomes an active, collective factor of progress.

People who have lived through the same experience, the same upheavals, can be said to bear a 'common imprint', in the apt phrase of Marc Bloch. The concept of *generation* takes on historical and political meaning to the extent that it underscores the significance of *collective experience.* The mechanical Marxist refuses – in the name of the class struggle – to take into consideration the significance of membership in a common generation. Yet the Chinese Cultural Revolution stressed the active role of such experience. One of its concrete aims was to pass on the torch of the revolution to the new generation, bypassing the stratum of managers who had assumed leadership of a socialism handed to them on a silver platter by the revolutionary generation that preceded them. Such was the basic meaning of the appeal to the 'Red Guards'. The opposite side of the coin is the strange fate of those who have outlived the period of their historical and social relevance, of their 'common imprint' – for example, the widow of Napoleon III, Empress Eugénie, who bore a large individual responsibility for the French defeat at Sedan in the Franco-Prussian War of 1870 and died in 1922; or Kerensky, head of the ill-fated 'Provisional Government' overthrown by the Bolshevik Revolution, who died in New York in 1970, half a century later; or the last of the French Communards who died in the Soviet Union in 1942.

The historical flux is heterogeneous and frequently interrupted.

Cosmic time unfolds with the imperturbable regularity of the stars; 'civil' time parallels cosmic time in the days and years of the calendar. Real historical time, on the contrary, constantly expands and contracts. It is shaped by the trials and struggles of human beings.

Historical time, Soviet-style, stresses the automatic succession of five-year plans in a uniform, undifferentiated flux reflecting the constant growth of productive forces as the foundation of socialist construction. Historical time, Chinese-style, consists of advances and retreats, accelerations and stabilizations, sharp changes of tempo like the Great Leap Forward or the Cultural Revolution. It appeals to human initiative, gives priority to the political struggle as a means of mobilizing the energy of the people and emphasizes the varying degrees of resistance this mobilization encounters from the obstacles along its path.

The problem of the short run and the long run, of continuity and discontinuity, is basically a political problem. In saying this, we relegate to the background a whole series of recent intellectual debates on the question of the long-run time-span in history.

Fernand Braudel, for example, stresses the varying levels of protracted time-spans, depending on whether the viewpoint is commercial, demographic, cultural or technological — which means that there could be qualitatively different protracted time-spans ('temps longs'). In his study of the concept of history, Louis Althusser takes Braudel's pluralist thesis of qualitatively different 'temps longs' as his premise. Such Liberalism may appear surprising in so intransigent a Marxist expert, but it makes sense. It reflects the previously-mentioned convergence between the modernist and dogmatic versions of gradualist continuity as the basic fabric of history. Taking the apolitical plurality of various kinds of 'temps longs' for granted, he calls upon historians to establish the complex articulations among them, to arrange them in some kind of hierarchical order — and demonstrate the ultimately decisive role of the economic. Foucault's approach is different. While accepting, like Althusser, Braudel's concept of different kinds of 'temps longs', he draws a sharp distinction between 'global history' and 'general history' (see the Introduction to his *Archéologie du savoir*). The former yearns for the organic integration of various time-spans; the latter stresses the stubborn problem of series, interruptions, gaps, ups and downs, discrepancies, time-related characteristics, the unique effects of historical experience. One strives to relate everything to a 'single centre', while the other 'unfolds the space of a dispersion'.

Pluralism of 'temps longs', the 'complex articulation' of various past experiences, integration or dispersion — all these are certainly genuine problems. But they are meaningless apart from social practice. To discuss them without reference to ongoing struggles is once again standing the old historical rhetoric on its head. The point rather is to plant it squarely on its two feet, to root it in today's struggles.

The Chinese peasants know very well that they are passing from one period to another. For them, this historical reality is a 'coherent whole'. That basic fact transcends and unifies the 'complex articulation' of separate experiences they have lived through — quite varied experiences, in fact: centuries-old feudalism, the recent terrorism of the Guomindang, the subjection of women from time immemorial, imperialist exploitation since the nineteenth century. Here we have, undeniably, a 'plurality of protracted time-spans' — some longer than others. But *it is in the present that they can be brought together, unified* through a global transformation that is the culmination of each and envelops them all.

In France today the problem of the plurality of 'temps longs' and their articulation is basically political. For the Occitans, the long-range period, experienced as a period of struggle, goes back to the northern conquest of southern France in the thirteenth century. For women, it goes back to the neolithic era. For the workers, it coincides with the establishment of the factory system in the nineteenth century and its subsequent technical adaptations: the assembly-line, for example, or the eight-hour shift. For the residents of big cities, it corresponds to the development of the huge concrete housing projects of the twentieth century and, for the immigrant workers, to the decolonization crisis. While these struggles are frequently anchored in the distant past, they are united *in the present* by the common denominator of a single adversary — the capitalist system. Their distinct pasts — the 'plurality of protracted time-spans' again — are merged in a common present and in the struggle for a common future. How can all these distinct long-range experiences be brought together and united in a single explosive whole? That is a problem not for the 'practising historian' but for the 'makers of history' — the masses of people.

15 History 'from the top down' and grass-roots history: the role of the masses

The historian is more comfortable in upper-class company − some recent attempts to expand the historical field to include the 'little people' − an expansion, but not a reversal − the people make history, either passively or actively − criminality and human-interest stories − the masses, heroes, and vanguards − have women a history? − what kind?

Historically, history has developed 'from the top down'. Not only does historical knowledge serve the interests of the power structure and the ruling classes, but the rulers and upper circles are traditionally the favourite subjects of historical research and writing.

■ *Choice of subject:* Military, political and diplomatic history still claim priority, despite the attacks of the *Annales* group. Even biography, a field historians are especially fond of for its concreteness and its 'human side', concentrates almost exclusively on members of the ruling classes, since only they had the time to write letters or diaries, or were considered worth writing about as human beings. For example, the best textbook of Chinese history during the Manchu dynasty is the one entitled *Eminent Chinese of the Ching Period*; it was published in Washington in 1946 at a time when American policy-makers identified China with Tchang Kai-chek and other eminent Chinese of the Guomindang, and Max Weber's sociological theories of 'élites' were beginning to have an impact in the American universities.

■ *Nature of sources and their use:* It is almost always the rich and power-ful who leave materials behind, either individually or through various state organs and other power structures such as private commercial or industrial firms, religious orders, universities, etc. This is particularly true in the case of quantified materials.

■ *The description of mechanisms:* A bourgeois historian who frequents the *salons* and private clubs of the wealthy and moves among influential people naturally tends in his work to give priority to the political world to which he belongs. He attributes more importance, for example, to a prime minister's behind-the-scenes remarks than to a street demonstration. Such demonstrations, in his view, are merely the work of 'agitators'. He is

ignorant of what every militant knows so well – the problem of informing
the public, of writing effective leaflets, the delicate choice of an itinerary,
and the tormenting question: 'How many people will turn up?'

■ *Language:* The historian's language is that of other 'educated' intellectuals – in other words, the language of the bourgeoisie. But there is an
unspoken agreement among historians to ignore its class character and
to make of this language a test of neutrality and scientific objectivity,
even a sign of professional cohesiveness. And so we speak of 'disorders'
and 'agitators' – the terminology and ideology of the police. But it is
not considered 'objective' to speak of mass struggles. It is acceptable to
speak of 'diplomatic pressures' and 'economic penetration' – the language
of a board of directors or a corporation president. But it is a sign of 'bias'
to speak of colonialist terror or imperialist looting.

■ *Exclusions:* Those excluded from the political decision-making process
are also excluded from the history books. This applies to rebels and
marginal elements of all kinds. Conventional historians constantly refer
to ordinary people, the workers, as the 'anonymous' mass, a favourite
term in the mouths of those who set great store by 'name', as in the
phrase 'to make a name for oneself'. The same is true for women. A
recent survey of secondary school textbooks in France showed that
women play a very limited role in conventional French history, usually
as occasional stars – like Blanche de Castille the mother, Joan of Arc the
warrior, Madame Rolland the intellectual – as domestic servants ('The
serf's wife takes care of the house,' the average textbook informs us),
or as hysterical shrews like the women marchers on Versailles in the
French Revolution of 1789, or the Revolutionary women of the 1871
Commune, branded as 'incendiaries' (*pétroleuses*) by the bourgeoisie.

Recently, a number of professional historians have made an effort to
overcome the conventional bias of their profession in favour of the
upper classes. Their attempts concern the means of information and
methods of research. The use of popular traditions, of imagery, of
'literary' sources such as novels, private correspondence, even opinion
polls for the recent period really do enable them to surmount, at least
partially, the obstacle of reliance on 'first-hand documents' exclusively
controlled by the powers-that-be. As a result, we can learn more easily
about the life of the masses of people in the past. The effort to demo-
cratize history also influences the choice of subjects previously ignored –
e.g., the phenomena of collective consciousness (fear, forgetfulness,
memory, irrational impulses); the life of the common people (work
techniques, attitudes, popular culture – although all this is often approached from a depoliticized 'long-range' perspective); forms of resistance and struggle (marginalism, banditry, prison life, prostitution, as
well as peasant movements, workers' strikes, trade-union experience).

These new subjects are fashionable among the younger historians, but their positive attempts to expand the horizons of investigation end up by merely renovating academic history, giving it a new lease on life. Periodicals like *Le mouvement social* in France and *Peasant Studies* in England respect the imperatives of the historian's professional rhetoric – the cult of the quantitative, learned monographs, the priority of documentation as against problem-solving. So the exploited, the peasants and workers, are in their turn caught up in the academic machine through the intermediary of those who have taken them as their 'field', in line with the conventional emphasis of the university world on professional specialization.

All this is undoubtedly an improvement over the academic snobbishness of preceding generations. It is progress to break the spell of archives documentation, to defy bourgeois conformism and moralistic tabus, to seriously examine the past life of the masses of people. But there are definite reasons for the emergence of this new approach; the excluded ones have been banging vigorously at the doors of French history. Witness the rash of wildcat strikes, particularly since 1968, the peasants' roadblocks on the highways, the challenge of youth's counter-culture, the movements of prisoners, of prostitutes. But historical knowledge, even expanded to include the masses in its scope of interest, is democratic only in form, for it remains external to us; in the name of academic custom and unavoidable compromise, it excludes active commitment to the struggles of the present.

We must go further. We can no longer be satisfied to 'work' (another distortion of language, for work is defined by its social aims and utility) *on* peasant struggles, or *on* American utopian communities, to use the naive language of people's movement specialists, of young scholars preparing theses on marginal social groups, of researchers in Ann Arbor, Michigan, busily feeding into their computers all the data they can find on the incidence of strikes throughout French history – all with the help of their own crew of semi-skilled workers. What is needed, however, is the ability to work not *on* but *with* the workers, the peasants, the people, and that is much more difficult than to remain inside the university world and try to achieve a success of sorts with an 'original', 'stimulating' or 'suggestive' thesis; the mandarin vocabulary is sufficiently rich and elastic to cover any situation.

For the role of the masses of people in the development of historical knowledge depends on their role in the general course of history itself. What is really meant by the deceptively simple saying: 'It is the masses who make history'? How do they act and make their influence felt? In the first place, by working. The basic fabric of history is a product of the social organization of productive labour and it is as *producers*, as a labour force, that the masses of people exert their historical influence. In one of his more famous poems, Bertolt Brecht made the point that nothing can happen in history without the people:

Questions from a worker who reads

Who built the town of Thebes of Seven Gates?
The names of kings are written in the books.
Was it the kings who dragged the slabs of rock?
And Babylon, so many times destroyed,
Who built her up again so many times? In what hovels
Did the workers of gold-glittering Lima live?
Where did the masons go the night the Chinese wall
Was finished? Great Rome
Is full of arches of triumph. Who raised them? Over whom
Did Caesars triumph? In Byzantium, much-praised in song,
Were all the houses palaces? Even in fabulous Atlantis,
The night she sank into the sea,
The drowning masters must have bellowed for their slaves.

Young Alexander conquered India.
All by himself?
Caesar beat the Gauls.
Not even a cook to help him with his meals?
Philip of Spain wept loud when his Armada
Went down. Did no one else weep?
Frederick the Great won the Seven Years War. Who
Else was the winner?

On every page a triumph.
Who baked the victory cake?

In every decade a great man.
Who picked up the check?

So many reports.
So many questions.

More often than not, the countless anonymous artisans of victories and monuments pass for loyal, obedient supporters of the established order. For the masses of people *do* accept the existing system for long periods of time, or at least put up with it. They are subjected to its economic laws and integrated into its prevailing relations of production. At the same time, they acknowledge its political power structure and internalize its values. This consensus, this social inertia, is in some cases extremely pronounced. It may be based on irrational behaviour patterns, as Maria Macciocchi pointed out with reference to the acceptance of Mussolini's fascism by the Italian women: to compensate psychologically for 'intolerable' living conditions, they blindly put their faith in the fascist doctrine, in the fatherland, in the leader, in the male power-symbol to whom millions obediently turned over their golden wedding-rings during the war in Ethiopia. It would be a mistake to close our eyes to the mass support enjoyed by De Gaulle, by Hitler, by Napoleon and other wielders of highly personalized power. The ideological oppression of the workers — their domination by the ideas of the ruling class — is no less intense than their economic oppression. And anyone who refuses to recognize this as a reality both today and throughout human history is certain to have some unpleasant surprises.

Yet the power structure also arouses the resistance of the people, although that resistance is often latent, or merely individual in its form of expression. It runs the gamut of marginalism and insubordination from the 'unproductive' artisan or peasant who stubbornly rejects the economic imperatives of capitalist society to the young hippy, from the worker who constantly changes jobs 'for no valid reason' to the 'eccentric old man' who does not care how funny people think he is. The people's rejection of conventional values is also expressed through all the forms of criminality, of disrespect for property rights and the rules of 'good conduct'. This was the message of Georges Darien's novel *Le Voleur* and George Jackson's *Soledad Brother*. Malingering in the factories, minor sabotage, deliberate spoiling of work — all are aspects of this vast outpouring of rejection and protest. Such delinquency belongs to the way of life of the oppressed — it is a kind of rebellion. Similarly, the criminality of the rich (or the would-be rich) is an expression of their greed, an unheroic short-cut path up the social ladder. Jean Valjean and Al Capone are the epitome of two contradictory forms of criminality. The same class boundaries run across 'polite society' and the underworld.

Is criminality political? Yes, since it is a rebellion against the power structure, the state and its laws. No, since it is individualistic behaviour inspired by the basic principle of capitalism: line your own pockets with a minimum of effort. A robbery does not challenge that fundamental principle. It is therefore less different — despite appearances to the contrary — from a normal purchase transaction than is, for example, an act of collective expropriation like the one carried out in 1973 by the workers of the Lip watch factory in France when they confiscated the watches stocked in the plant which they were occupying illegally in order to finance their strike.

All the forms of individual resistance to the power structure belong to the experience of daily life and provide the press with many a human interest story. Such stories, carefully interpreted and divested of their false sensationalism, are rich in political and historical lessons. This is true for the human interest stories both of today and of the past. Beneath the apparently fortuitous circumstances surrounding them, we discern the basic contradictions of the society as revealed in a street fight, a family quarrel, an 'accident' that is anything but accidental, miscellaneous 'crimes and misdemeanours'. An historical collection of human interest stories would tell us as much about a particular period as many a scholarly compilation of documents and material.

Examples are rare of direct, collective action by the masses of people, decisively upsetting the existing power structure and bringing the latent contradictions of society to the boiling point. It happened in France in 1789 and 1793, in China in 1911, in Russian in 1917, in China again between 1937 and 1949. Often such sudden, direct outbreaks of mass action take the 'leaders', the administrators, the organizations, completely by surprise. Sun Yat-sen learned of the fall of the Chinese empire in Denver, Colorado; John Reed did not try to conceal the joyous disorder of the 'Ten Days That Shook the World'; not a single militant vanguard organization or group of leaders predicted the Paris explosion of May '68.

But the role of the people in history is not limited to spectacular outbreaks. No discussion of the people's *continuous* capacity to influence the course of history can avoid examining the possible circumstances under which such influence can be exerted either directly or through individuals or organizations who become the spokesmen of the people and assume authority in their name. The relationship of the masses of people to leading individuals and to vanguard groups are key problems of the present and the past alike.

The problem of 'heroes' in history is one of the classical themes of Marxist thought. It has been the subject of many a famous debate from the time of Lenin and Plekhanov to that of Liu Shao-qi and the Red Guards. An article in the *Peking Review* of 21 July 1972 expressed it in these terms:

> . . . heroes exert a considerable influence on quickening or slowing down the making of history by the masses. However, they can change the tempo but not change the direction of historical progress. Heroes are born of revolutionary struggles and can play their role only when they are with the masses. Advanced ideas and theories are a reflection of the demand of the masses for revolution and an epitome of the experience in struggle; they will become a material force advancing history only when they are grasped by the masses.

This analysis is confirmed by the fact that the strict correspondence between the interests of the people and the aims of the 'heroes' rarely continues throughout their entire career. Exceptional political careers usually consist of alternating phases of withdrawal and preeminence. As a result, bourgeois historians, obsessed by 'strong personalities' and 'out-standing characters', wonder how 'mediocre' people can rise unexpectedly to positions of top leadership and responsibility, how 'geniuses' can suddenly drop out of the limelight, why people of extraordinary ability were not discovered earlier, etc. These alternating phases characterize the careers of such political leaders as Thiers and De Gaulle, Sun Yat-sen

and Gandhi, Churchill and Truman. The action of individuals, whether
in the service of the ruling classes or the revolutionary mass movement, is
typically *ephemeral* and *discontinuous*. Precisely when and under what
circumstances does the activity of an individual correspond to the underlying currents of history? At what point, and by what mechanisms, does
this correspondence disappear?

But Marxist literature is far less explicit concerning the relationship
between the masses of people and the vanguard groups. More often than
not, they — meaning the self-appointed vanguards — simply take it for
granted that the people can act effectively only by delegating their
historical mission to specially qualified leading groups. Usually, they
rationalize their attitude by resorting to metaphors: the fish and the
sea, the plant-roots and the soil, the pianist and the keys he plays upon.
The Little Red Book offers a whole collection of these. But the fish (or
the pianist, or the root) is always external to the masses of people. How
can this limitation be transcended? Unqualified spontaneity has failed.
In any case, the definition of the Party as an absolute vanguard was
carried furthest by Lenin and Stalin. 'We Communists are people of a
special mould,' said Stalin at Lenin's grave in 1924. But such a concept
is nearly absent from the writings of Marx, from the *Manifesto* to the
Civil War in France. One of the most valuable contributions of the
Chinese Cultural Revolution was to have divested the 'Party', temporarily at least, of its unchallengeable role and its aura of infallibility.

Can we conceive of a history produced by the masses of people in
terms of their own needs? A history that would assign professional historians the role of useful auxiliaries rather than privileged custodians of
wisdom? Experimental attempts along these lines have already been made.
In the United States, there is a 'guerrilla history' just as there is a 'guerrilla
theatre' — a flexible, mobile approach to the past that is based on concrete needs unhampered by the rigid requirements of conventional scholarship and couched in terms that can be understood by everyone. Such an
approach was tried out in working-class neighbourhoods of Chicago
around 1970. And in China between 1960 and 1965, people were urged
to practise 'the four histories' — village history, family history, factory
history, people's communes history. Local experiences, memories, traditions, written records — all were collected at the grass-roots in order to
assess the recent past and the stakes of socialism. The people's past was
an instrument of the people's struggle.

But it is for the people, not the professional historians, to evaluate
this weapon and define its uses. It is for women themselves to determine
how the record of their past can contribute to their present struggles. One
approach would be, for example, to find inspiration in certain key events
like the American strikes of the nineteenth century or in vanguard figures

of the revolutionary upheavals of 1848 and 1871 in France like Flora Tristan or Louise Michel. Or women could take a long, hard look at what Maria Macciocchi has called the 'a-historic' monotony of their condition throughout the centuries, the constant repetition, from one generation to the next, of burdens and humiliations: 'That's how it was for your grandmother — and for her grandmother before her!' Women have a long way to go to shift from 'history' to 'herstory'.*

Reflecting on the possibility of a history that would no longer be the special province of professional historians but the possession of the people means raising the more fundamental question of the type of society in which we want to live. But it is also a way of contributing to the solution of that problem.

* *Herstory* is the title of an annual published by women in New Zealand.

5 The pace of development: the ups and downs of history

ogress' as the ideology of the bourgeoisie – the passage from one ode of production to another is a complicated process – gaps, blocks, ke-offs, contrasting environments – transference of models, resurgences, ort-cuts, survivals – Romein's law of the retarding lead – progress, re-ession, relapse – is there a point of no return in history?

e nineteenth-century bourgeoisie identified its own ambitions, its own terests, its own future, with the course of history itself. The concept *progress* as an absolute was the ideological foundation of liberal pitalism. In the twentieth century, the idea of progress as the inherent rward movement of human societies, as a superior motive force, re-ains one of the axioms of imperialism's technicist ideology. This is rticularly true in the field of economic theory: W. W. Rostow, President nnedy's adviser, is the author of the 'take-off' thesis, the basis of all ficial American studies of the 'under-developed countries'. Kennedy ed the expression 'Alliance for Progress' to describe the system of wer and exploitation imposed by the United States in Latin America. rogress' justifies imperialism and provides a ready-made criterion by ich to judge a society or a social class in terms of the dominant model development. Expressions like 'You can't stand in the way of progress!' 'It's the law of progress!' constitute a supposedly unanswerable argu-ent – one that the people themselves have largely accepted and inter-lized.

The same historical optimism, the same certitude of a progressive and interrupted improvement of living conditions for the human race, ve at various times penetrated classical Marxism. This was particularly e for the revisionism of the Second International and the writings of rnstein, as well as for the Stalinist theory of the 'five stages'. Such storical optimism was not absent from the thinking of Karl Marx.

In reality, the general movement of history is far more complex. What e principle of progress really means is that, in the long run – but in e long run only – all human societies are *capable* of progressively freeing themselves, which is quite different from the conception of automatic progress regardless of what happens along the way.

'The ascent of man from the kingdom of necessity to the kingdom of freedom!' The process of progressive liberation summarized in Engel's famous phrase takes place through a succession of social forms linked to one another by bonds of historical necessity. Capitalism contains in germ the preconditions of socialism, not those of slavery; the realization of those preconditions is another matter. Each such stage is more advanced in quality, not merely in time, than the preceding one. Progress is not a straight line. Capitalism is definitely an advance over slavery, for it means a degree of personal freedom, a better control over the conditions of life and death, wider horizons and possibilities. But precisely because it prepares the path for socialism, and at the same time opposes its coming, capitalism employs forms of exploitation much more sophisticated than those of slavery or feudalism, as well as new and superior forms of oppression. It has made progress in the art of imprisoning people, both materially and morally, and in the art of 'controlling and punishing', to borrow Michel Foucault's apt phrase. Here lie the roots of the old 'Golden Age' myth and of the nostalgia for the past that is prevalent in every class society, including our own. The 'progress' achieved under capitalism is basically only *potential* and has no meaning unless it *actually leads to socialism.* Until now, such potentialities have been stifled by the weight of the enormous apparatus of oppression and exploitation that capitalism has set up to maintain its power. Compare, for example, the successive war machines of Alexander the Great's army, the army of the Crusaders, Napoleon's army, the army of the Pentagon.

The modes of production and the socio-economic forms of organization as defined by Marxist theory are abstract models. And as abstract models they are indispensable. In reality, however, passage from one system to another is not a mechanical process. Concrete history is *unfinished, incomplete.* It consists of detours, gaps, obstacles, take-offs, short-cuts, survivals, reversals – and even of regressions and retreats.

The study of these complex phenomena has been consistently overlooked by narrowly specialized historians. They have abandoned it to the 'philosophers of history' in the worst sense of the word – the practitioners of empty rhetoric, babbling for page on end about the tumultuous March of Time; they are a declining species. Yet these phenomena are particularly significant, since they constitute the very warp and woof of the world in which we live – the world we must not only *understand* but also *change.* The problem of historical regression is raised with special acuteness today, as is the problem of historical short-cuts for the Third World, and of cultural survivals and resurgences in such areas as Brittany and among the American Indians. It is therefore useful to study these phenomena as they have occurred in the past — in order to gain mastery over them in the present.

Historical development is *uneven*. The classical itinerary of class societies from slavery to capitalism is observable only in the Mediterranean region and in Western Europe, and even there we find exceptions. Vast areas have long remained outside this line of development. Thus, the 'Asiatic societies' evolved belatedly towards a specific form of feudalism, which was turned inwards and incapable of developing by itself into societies with private capitalism as their mainspring. Or the 'Barbarian Kingdoms' of the early Middle Ages in northern and northwestern Europe: Scandinavia and what are today the British Isles. Or the marginal societies of Oceania and Amazonia. Among these societies we find complex phenomena of *cultural gap* — gaps often expressed by *blocks* and *stagnation*, at least for a middle-range period of time, but also by spectacular *take-offs*, such as the 'Greek miracle' that left the other ancient societies far behind, the Industrial Revolution that put Great Britain ahead of the other countries of the feudal West, socialist Cambodia in the Third World. At present there is a definite *gap* between India and China, a quarter of a century after liberation processes that were quite different in the two countries.

This uneven development is also a *combined development*. The gaps are the expression of *contrasting environments* that are historically necessary for the development and even the survival of a given society. Greco-Roman slavery could exist only at the expense of a 'Barbarian' ('Asiatic') environment not based on slavery but constituting a vast reservoir of slaves — the relation between the two was a *structural necessity* for Greece and Rome. The ancient world collapsed when the Barbarians entered the City — the capture of Rome took place in AD 410. As for capitalism, it could not survive except by exploiting a largely non-capitalist environment in which it finds raw materials, labour, export markets; the 'underdevelopment' of the Third World is, for capitalism, another *structural necessity*. But this was not the case for feudalism, which was capable of surviving and developing on its own 'home grounds' on the basis of the lingering tribal society of ancient Germany or the superficially Romanized society of Gaul. From this point of view, feudalism is qualitatively different from other class societies. Slavery, historically older, seems more 'modern' qualitatively. One more good reason to reject the Stalinist 'five-stage' concept of mechanical, unilinear development.

Uneven development also enables us to understand the failure of all attempts at *transference of models*. It is futile to try to impose artificially upon a particular type of society patterns borrowed from the collective experience of a different type of society, with the aim of shaping the former on the model of the latter. The graft is rejected! This failure was experienced by the Greek colonies in the Barbarian Mediterranean, by the Latin States of Syria in the Middle Ages, by the institutions of French feudalism transplanted to Canada, by British parliamentarianism in the former colonies of Great Britain following independence by the Soviet bureaucracy in China in the 1950s.

Uneven and combined development also creates the possibility of a *resurgence* of various historical forces following long periods of *hibernation*. The Indians of the United States, like the Melanesians of New Caledonia, were supposedly wiped off the slate of history until the middl of the twentieth century. Today, they are displaying renewed energy as capitalist society shows signs of splitting apart. Acupuncture, recently revived in China, was in hibernation throughout the period of the 'unequal treaties' when the country was under the sway of the Western cultural model and the accompanying advantages offered the 'modern' Chinese doctors in Shanghai and other open ports. But such *resurgence* is out of the question unless the social forces in question have remained above a certain threshold. The Aborigines of Australia made a comeback, but it was too late for the Tasmanians, victims of large-scale genocide. The threshold concept applies to both camps — the colonizers and the colonized alike. Thus, the colonial domains of Holland and Portugal managed to revive after the Napoleonic Wars and survived into the nineteenth century, but not those of Denmark and Sweden, which were too scanty to develop further and advance from trading-posts to empires.

Uneven and combined development also creates the possibility of *short cuts*. Certain peoples have been able to go directly to socialism, bypassing the capitalist phase, by reason of their inclusion in larger political entities capable of promoting such a transition — for example, Tibet and Mongolia. Or by reason of the high political level of their struggle, enabling them to 'skip stages' — North Vietnam and Cambodia.

The prevailing mode of production does not always manage to impose its economic principles mechanically on the entire social fabric; and it is not always opportune for it to do so. The prevailing relations are often combined with *survivals* from a preceding period. At times it strives to eliminate such survivals, as was the case with the France of the Fifth Republic, a latecomer to the age of monopoly capitalism. Sometimes, on the contrary, there is an attempt to integrate them in order to reinforce the prevailing system; for example, capitalist Great Britain has preserved the feudal institutions of the monarchy, and slavery was artificially kept alive in the capitalist United States of the eighteenth and nineteenth centuries.

But survivals also work in the opposite direction. They can become centres of resistance to the dominant mode of production – a contradictory role since they both prolong the past and provide the point of departure for new directions. The crisis of the nation-state in the capitalist West is characterized by the revival of minority groups which, in the absence of a theoretical analysis of this new phenomenon, are temporarily defined as 'national'. The Scots, the Indians of the United States, the Bretons, the Sardinians, the Chicanos, the Occitans – all base their identity on their long past. But if they are to avoid reproducing on a small scale the model of the nation-state against which they are rising, they will have to define their situation as that of a transition towards a new and socialist society. The usual roles of the 'advanced' and the 'backward' have been reversed.

More generally speaking, the sector that is most advanced at a particular stage of development may prove least capable of making the transition to another stage governed by different economic principles. It is handicapped by its own advancement and the *overload* it entails. Certain 'Asiatic' societies like Egypt were unable to maintain their initial 'advance' (as exemplified, for example, by their huge waterworks) over the tribal societies of Greece and Italy, which were the first to pass to slavery, a more developed form of society. In an article written in 1913, Lenin spoke of 'backward Europe and advanced Asia' but in a different sense; he was contrasting the people's revolutions under way in the East at the beginning of the twentieth century with the conservatism of the capitalist countries of the West. Herzen had earlier formulated, in a more general sense, the concept of 'latecomers' who enjoy the historical advantage of their own 'backwardness':

Nothing in Russia bears the mark of routine, stagnation, inevitability that is encountered in nations which, through a long and painful process, have managed to create forms of social life that more or less correspond to their conceptions. Do not forget that Russia has not yet experienced the three scourges that have held back the development of the West: Catholicism, Roman law and the rule of the bourgeoisie. And we have no reason to repeat the epic of your emancipation; it has cluttered your path with so many monuments of the past that you are barely able to make the slightest progress. Your labours and your sufferings serve you as lessons; history is very unjust. The latecomers receive, not an already nibbled bone, but the best seats at the table of experience. The entire course of historical development is nothing but an *expression of time's ingratitude.* *

Chernishevsky expressed the same idea with an equally vivid figure of speech:

'History is like a grandmother: *She loves her youngest children best.* To

* See J. Lentz, *De La Russie et de l'Amérique*, Paris 1971.

the latecomers, she gives not the bones but the marrow of the bones that Western Europe has been ruining her fingers in an attempt to break.'

Mao Ze-dong expressed the same idea with his image of China as an empty page. In the old 'advanced' countries like France or the United States, cluttered with the debris of their setbacks, the paths to socialism are often particularly slow and tortuous. All this can be summed up in the 'law of the retarding lead' put forward around 1930 by the Dutch historian, J. Romein. W. F. Wertheim, in his *East–West Parallels* provides this paraphrase of Romein's work, which is available only in Dutch:

> . . . far from developing in a gradual way, human history progresses by leaps and bounds, comparable to the mutations known from the world of living nature. A next step in human evolution is not at all likely to occur within the society which has achieved a high degree of perfection in a given direction. On the contrary, the progress once achieved in the past is liable to act as a brake upon further progress. Both an atmosphere of complacency and vested interests tend to oppose further steps which might involve a complete overhaul of established institutions or equipments.
>   Therefore, further progress on the road of human evolution is, time and again, much more likely to occur in a more backward society, where resistances against social change are weaker. Romein shows that leadership in human evolution perpetually shifts from one society to another, after over-specialization has led yesterday's leader into a blind alley. . . . A few of his most striking illustrations of his thesis are the following: delay in the introduction of electric lighting in London, which was the first city to develop illumination with gas and to carry it forth to remarkable perfection; the lagging behind of the productivity of collieries in Britain, France and Belgium, the countries which were the first to develop large-scale coal mining; the advantages of latecomer Japan over Britain as far as modernization is concerned; and finally the occurrence of the proletarian revolution in backward Russia contrary to the prophecies of those Marxists who had expected this revolution to take place in Germany, at that time industrially the most developed country. The general design of his argument is to show that backwardness may, under certain circumstances, act as an advantage and a spur to further effort, whereas rapid advance in the past may act as a brake. This is what he calls the 'dialectics of progress', or 'the law of the retarding lead'.

Progress is therefore neither unilinear nor inevitable. Entire societies have gone out of existence: like Angkor, overrun by jungle; or the Mayan cities; or Nichapoor, capital of Tamerlane's empire, today a little town on the desert trail – between Teheran and Meshed, it is hardly noticed.

Progress itself applies only to certain sectors of the society at the expense of others. Large-scale industry ruthlessly eliminates small-scale production. Examples: the British peasants; the Indian weavers ('whose bones whiten the plains of the Ganges', wrote an English Governor at the beginning of the nineteenth century, in a Biblical vein); the little trades that once flourished on the streets of Paris; the Russian handicrafts, liquidated under Stalin and later revived for the tourist trade to bring in foreign currency. All of which is taken for granted and written off as the 'price of progress'!

But as Illich points out, it takes fourteen times more energy to harvest a ton of wheat today than it did in the Middle Ages. On the one hand: a horse, its feed, and what it takes to produce it, simple tools and the foundry where they are made. On the other hand an interminable list: fertilizer, silos, machines, fuel and the whole cycle of activities involved in their production.

The choice between progress and regression arises only within a particular societal organization. Societies that have reached a certain level of development, at least in appearance, are in danger of relapsing into a previous type, if they have not achieved a sufficient degree of cohesion. Is there such a thing as a point of no return in history?

▪ Roman and Byzantine Asia minor, a society based first on slavery and then on feudalism, relapsed into the 'Asiatic' mode of production as a result of the Ottoman conquests at the end of the Middle Ages.

▪ All the pre-capitalist societies did not 'take off', as Great Britain did, or with the same continuity. Most of them seemed quite advanced along the path of the new capitalist mode of production by the end of the Middle Ages but fell back into feudalism after the sixteenth century: e.g., Bohemia, Venice and, to a certain extent, the Netherlands.

▪ Lenin was obsessed, at the beginning of the twentieth century, by the fear of an 'Asiatic restoration' (*aziachtchina*) in Russia.

▪ The socialist societies of Eastern Europe have relapsed into a new form of state capitalism based on the capture of the collective means of production by a bureaucratic neobourgeoisie recruited by co-optation.

▪ The 'unpublished' writings of Mao Ze-dong, especially those of the Cultural Revolution period, betray an obsession with the danger of similar relapses in China.

17 The space dimension in history: geopolitics

*Geographic factors have an impact within a particular mode of produc-
tion – insularity, 'continentality', contiguity – the principle of correspondence between the content of a phenomenon and its favourable
location – the shift of the centre of gravity of workers' struggles
according to the stakes involved – the cases of Germany, Great Britain,
China – since May '68, Paris has learned to 'follow the lead of the
provinces'*

The gaps, blocks and environmental contrasts discussed above all exist
in space. They are *geopolitical* manifestations.

The word geopolitics frightens people – it has had a bad press. In the
nineteenth century, it was used by the geographers of German imperialism
like Ratzel. In their view, each country's natural configuration condemns
its people to an inexorable destiny. Planted firmly in the heart of Europe,
Germany's destiny was to dominate the continent; and Russia, an endless
plain, was naturally fated to be conquered time and again by forces to the
west and the east.

It is, of course, ridiculous to regard geographical realities as decisive
in the last analysis, but it is no less ridiculous to be satisfied with a blanket
rejection of such crude geographical determinism. Space is an objective
fact, and history's spatial dimension involves a complex set of relationships.
Geography exerts a real, concrete influence; it shapes development, setting
its direction and limits. This geographic influence is *relative* to a given
mode of production and its basic economic principles.

■ The shape of the plains and mountains along the eastern coasts of the
Indochinese peninsula set the pattern for the 'march to the south' (*Nam-
Tien*) of Vietnamese peasants throughout the centuries, and in this way
gave a precise shape to the national territory – swollen at the deltas of
both extremities, narrow and distended at the centre where the mountains
nearly join the sea. But this configuration was decisive only within the
general framework of the laws governing the mode of production in

Vietnam — the 'Asiatic' form of feudalism based on autonomous villages and the public irrigation of the plains.

■ The continued isolation of Bohemia was largely responsible for its 'blocked' condition ever since the sixteenth century, although at the end of the Middle Ages the buds of an emerging capitalism were already highly developed, with mines and factories, large commercial firms, a scientific and technological upsurge in which scholars from all over Europe participated, a spurt of intellectual and religious radicalism marked by the rise of the Hussites. Bohemia's continental position was a heavy handicap at the dawn of capitalism during a phase of economic development when long-distance trade by sea (e.g., the case of Great Britain) was virtually indispensable to the primitive accumulation of capital, to getting expanded reproduction under way. With the advent of railroads, Bohemia's continental location ceased to be an obstacle to the development of Czech heavy industry. The impact of natural factors is conditional, then, on the particular socio-economic organization. When the economic base changes, these geographic factors continue to play — but in a different direction.

■ Take the phenomenon of *insularity*. The favourable geographic position of ancient Greece ceased to be an asset during the era of Turkish predominance. Great Britain benefited from her insular location from the sixteenth century onward, but Japan was unable to do so until the Meiji revolution of 1868 broke its ancient feudal state structures. The coaling stations of the British empire were planted all along the maritime routes of the nineteenth century to supply the steamers that plied the 'seven seas'. It was the period of Britain's 'insular monopoly', so admired by the visionary Fourier. But these innumerable islands and ports of call lost their value in the age of fuel navigation.

■ Or take the phenomenon of *continentality*. China has been described somewhat rashly as shut in by the massive continental structure that condemned her to historical stagnation. As a matter of fact, Chinese history oscillates between periods when, depending on the economic context, relations either by sea or by land predominated, politically and economically speaking.

By land, in the era of the classical dynasties, including the Mongol period, which opened up a vast continental expanse. By sea, during the Ming era (fourteenth to seventeenth centuries), marked by the 'discovery' of Africa long before the Portuguese and by the beginnings of Chinese immigration into Southeast Asia. By land again, with the voluntary retreat of the Manchu dynasty, the 'closing up' of a China that was concerned about the danger of Western penetration and anxious to avoid the fate of India which she knew well. By sea, once again, in the age of imperialism, of unequal treaties, of great 'open doors' like Shanghai.

By land, during the period of the capitalist blockade and of close collaboration with the Soviet Union. By sea, since the break with Moscow — this time in the direction of the Third World, not the West alone.

■ Or the question of *contiguity*. The border does not function in the same way in a feudal as in a capitalist economy. In the former case, there is a zone of commercial and human exchanges with an indefinite political status; local sovereignties span the mountain ranges (e.g., the counts of Foix and the kings of Navarre, the counts of Savoy, the little Ardennes principalities). This is what the geographers call a 'border zone'. In the latter case, we find a definite *borderline*, strictly drawn to meet the state's expanded demands — close supervision of residents and migrants for purposes of police control and taxation, enforcement of military obligations, claims on underground resources, distinct monetary systems; every square meter, every individual, is assigned to the jurisdiction of one state or the other.

In the same way, the contiguity between China and Vietnam was decisive in the feudal era, enabling Vietnam to be integrated into the Confucian world. In the colonial period, the neighbouring areas between China and Vietnam were no longer more than a low-pressure zone as far as their historical dynamics were concerned, apart from very marginal and occasional contacts between Chinese and Vietnamese revolutionaries. At that time, most of colonial Vietnam's contacts with the outside world took place by sea and were directed towards metropolitan France and the capitalist world market. But in the era of contemporary liberation wars, the situation was reversed. Already during the war against French colonialism, around 1950, and even more so during the American escalation beginning in 1965, the northern border of Vietnam played a vital role by establishing a link between the Vietnamese people and their 'great rear': China.

Generally speaking, contiguity or the advantage of having a base of support or at least the benevolent neutrality of a friendly neighbour across the border, has proven to be a basic geopolitical principle for the revolutionary wars of the mid-twentieth century. 'Internal factors' undoubtedly take priority; a revolutionary war is rooted in the people's will to struggle. But the Algerian National Liberation Front enjoyed the support of Tunisia and Morocco; the Red Khmers could count on Vietnam and southern Laos; the guerrilla fighters of northeast Thailand could count on China, and the revolutionary Pathet Lao could rely on North Vietnam. They all knew they could find, on the other side of the border, a sheltered area for their training camps, a supply base and an opportunity to communicate with the outside world. These possibilities existed because the relationship of diplomatic forces on a world scale prevented the repressive troops of the enemy from pursuing them into their 'sanctuaries'. When the Soviet Union closed its borders in 1946 to the revolutionaries of Azerbaidjan in exchange for a hypothetical Soviet oil concession in northern Iran – a concession that the Shah skilfully permitted to wither away – the result was the massive slaughter of the Azerbaidjan communists, with tens of thousands of deaths at Tabriz. And when Tito broke with the Cominform in 1948, he sealed the doom of the Greek *Andartes*, the left-wing partisan fighters who until then could fall back on the Yugoslav mountains.

Historical processes always take place, then, under specific, concrete geographic conditions that vary from country to country and region to region. They mature most completely in the areas that offer the most appropriate economic, political and social conditions. This is *the principle of the correspondence between the economic and political content of an historical phenomenon and its geographical location*. That principle is no more than the concrete application of the concept of overdetermination in history. A general contradiction operates under concrete, overdetermined conditions and finds expression in a very specific *location*.

- Portuguese India consisted of trading posts established in the rich commercial cities of southern India: Goa, Calicut, Mysore. British India, on the other hand, had its main bases further to the north – Bombay, Calcutta, Delhi; for this type of penetration reflected the specific economic content of a British colonial empire that was interested in establishing bases on the continent, not merely along the coasts, with a view to industrial development.

- The little coastal ports in the centre of Vietnam – Benthuy, Faifo, Quinhon – played a key role in Vietnamese national life during the feudal period; they provided a chain of commercial and political relays between the great deltas of the Red River in the north and the Mekong in the south. But, from the nineteenth century onwards, these ports were neglected and fell into disuse under the colonial capitalist economy that was entirely oriented toward the areas linked to the world market, mainly Saigon and Haiphong.

- The most active Italian ports in the Byzantine era and the early Middle Ages were those located in the south, like Amalfi. Subsequently, the centre of gravity of Italian life shifted to the north, towards Pisa, Genoa, Venice, with the upsurge of proto-capitalism and its active long-distance trade. Later the centre of activity shifted further up the Po, an area better adapted to modern large-scale industry. The south went to sleep like the Neapolitan nobleman Don Cesare in Roger Vailland's novel, *The Law*. The principle of correspondence between an economic reality and its main location in space is strictly applicable to the entire history of the great Italian cities.

- The China that was 'useful' to the West in the mid-nineteenth century, because it offered the most lucrative field of activity, was the China of tea and silk in the southeast where the five ports forced open by the Opium War were located. In the age of financial imperialism a half-century later, the foreign financiers, promoters of mines and railroads, settled in the north. As late as 1950, the five ports that had been in operation ever since 1842 either had no railroad at all or were served only by small local lines.

So much for the correspondence between the content of economic development and the centres where it is successively localized as a result of shifts and slow migrations. *The same is true for political and social contradictions, for the class struggle.* There we find the same shifts, the same migrations. At each stage of historical development, the centre of gravity of the main contradiction, its principal location, shifts to the point where it is sharpest, most *meaningful*, most *operational*. In Peking, the point is often made that in 1830 the centre of the labour movement was located in England, with the rise of the Chartist movement; it was there that uncontrolled capitalist industrialization had proceeded furthest since the beginning of the nineteenth century, and it was there that the class struggle between workers and employers was most intense, with direct and brutal confrontations. Towards the middle of the nineteenth century, the international centre of the labour movement, the locus of the most advanced forms of struggle, shifted to France. It was there that the political struggles were most radical, the revolutions most frequent. In France, the class struggle of the workers assumed a clearly political dimension; it was there that the new question of political power was raised most acutely with the revolutionary upsurge of 1848, and the Paris Commune of 1871. Under the influence of the Second International and its social democracy, the centre of gravity, the high-pressure area, shifted to Germany; the eyes of the entire world labour movement were turned on that country in admiration. In terms of the reformist, parliamentary objectives of the Second International at that time, it was Germany that offered the best example of a powerful Social-Democratic Party, the largest number of trade unions and socialist newspapers, the most impressive financial reserves and strike chests, the strongest delegations of deputies in Parliament. But 1917 destroyed the political options on which the predominance of the German Social-Democrats had been based. With the birth of the Comintern in 1919, the principal pole of the labour movement shifted to Moscow. All the tensions of the post-war world were concentrated in the Bolshevik revolution, the result of an 'overdetermined' contradiction. In the aftermath of the Second World War, the struggles of the oppressed peoples came to the fore and the victories of Chinese Communism put Peking in a favourable and central position. The impact of People's China, both in the industrialized West and in the 'tempest zone' of the Third World, has been tremendous.

The Soviet Union in the heroic period of Bolshevism, and China after liberation, were genuine 'centres' in that they were real focal points of the basic international contradictions of the era. But such 'centres of contradictions' have a tendency to become 'centres of decision'. This is what happened in the Soviet Union with the Stalinized Comintern. In China, an attempt to set up a new 'International' took place just after the break with Moscow when Peng Chen and Liu Shao-qi steered Peking's foreign policy in that direction. In his last 'unpublished writings', Mao warned against the danger of such an institutionalization:

'In the middle of the twentieth century, the centre of the world revolution is China; in the future it will, *of course*, shift . . .' (italics added).

The same shifts, the same itinerant and migratory movements, can be observed on the scale of a single country. The centre of gravity of mass struggles, the spot where they reach the highest level of intensity and command the attention of the entire nation, shifts along with the stakes involved in these struggles, their social and political content.

In Great Britain at the beginning of the nineteenth century, London — with its aggressive artisans and its militant, visionary intellectuals like William Blake — was the locus of the most radical struggles. With the progress of industrialization, the Midlands — especially the big factories of Yorkshire and Lancashire — became the storm centre of labour conflicts. At the beginning of the twentieth century, it shifted north, to the industrial centres where capitalist exploitation was most intense: the Scottish Lowlands, where the strikes of 1917 in the shipyards along the Clyde took on near-revolutionary overtones. They marked the transition to the contemporary period; today the most militant struggles take place in those areas of the United Kingdom where social oppression is compounded by national aspirations, such as Northern Ireland, Wales, Scotland.

In the United States, we find the same shifts of activity from one area to another, reflecting historical developments. At the end of the nineteenth and the beginning of the twentieth century, the sharpest struggles took place in the north of the Great Plains, in Minnesota, in Wisconsin, in Illinois, as the result of the combination of a militant working class and a body of radical farmers, plus a strong dose of European socialism brought in by German and Scandinavian émigrés who were numerous in the area. This produced the powerful Chicago strikes over the eight-hour day and the farmer-labour populism that flourished under Governor LaFollette. During the 1930s, under the impact of the Depression, the workers of the big steel-mills and mines of the Middle West, mainly Ohio and Pennsylvania, were in the front lines. After the

World War and the Cold War, both of which froze all mass struggle in
the United States, the anti-capitalist forces emerged again in the 'sixties
around the Vietnam war issue and the crisis of capitalist society in
general. The radical intellectuals played an active role at the time, as did
the various ethnic minorities, such as the Blacks, the Indians, the Chicanos,
the Puerto Ricans. It was in California, New England and New York City
that the radical currents came together in a particularly dynamic way.
A few years earlier, before the rise of the New Left, the centre of activity
of the Left was in the South with the Civil Rights movement – the fight
for the rights of the oppressed Black people focused the democratic
aspirations of the entire country on the most conservative states of the
South, such as Alabama and Mississippi.

Geopolitical problems demand of the historian the same basic rethinking as do other aspects of historical knowledge. This means reversing the
past-present relationship, divesting the professionals of their privileges,
reorienting historical studies in terms of the questions raised by social
practice. The above-mentioned geopolitical considerations are neither
a flight into the picturesque past nor mere speculative rhetoric. They are
concerned with political strategy.

The Chinese Revolution is a particularly striking illustration of the
geopolitical mobility of struggles. In the 1924–27 period, the centre of
gravity shifted successively from Canton, Sun Yat-sen's red base, to
Shanghai, the heart of the working-class revolution, to Wuhan, focal point
of the last attempt to create a democratic united front. In each of these
cities in turn the struggle reached its highest level and assumed the most
advanced forms. The cadres and militants moved from one city to the
next in line with a particularly mobile strategy based on the diversity of
political and social conditions in those three main centres. The geopolitical switch from the 'Chinese soviets', set up in the south around 1930, to
the 'liberated zones' in the north around 1940 was even more basic; that
was precisely the meaning of the 'Long March'. This shift of the centre
of gravity over a distance of 3,000 kilometers reflected a basic change
in the content of the revolutionary struggle – a reversal of priorities. The
south offered the most propitious terrain for the struggle against the
Guomindang and its capital, Nanking, while the north was a more appropriate location for the armed struggle against the Japanese invaders. The
leaders of the Chinese Revolution constantly assessed and concretized
their strategy in geopolitical terms: 'China', said Mao, 'is one vast chess-
board.'

And France? Without going back to the French Revolution, it can be
observed that the struggles of the twentieth century have been distributed
in a very uneven, highly differentiated way over the various regions of the
country, according to the diversity of local conditions. For example, the

resistance against Napoleon III was strongest in the south and there it assumed the most radical forms — for months, armed struggle raged in the Lower Alps and the Var, and this is one of the forgotten pages in the history of French extra-Parliamentary political experience. The so-called 'Paris Commune' was also a phenomenon of Occitania, especially in Narbonne and other cities. It was the manifestation of a left-wing republicanism fired by the anti-centralist protest of Occitania. Even then, federalism was a phenomenon of the Left. Yet until recently all that was considered a thing of the past. It was generally assumed that the political life of France was forever frozen into the image of its rail-road maps — a rigid spider web with Paris at the centre. But the anti-Nazi resistance, and particularly the struggles of May '68, demonstrated the contrary.

Between 1942 and 1944, the big cities of the south, like Lyons and Toulouse, were much more active centres of resistance than Paris. The geopolitics of the underground armed struggle against the Germans revealed the ability of certain so-called 'backward regions' to play a vanguard role; this was true of such centres as the Ariège, the Limousin, the Jura, the Morvan. Another case of the 'retarding lead'. The Liberation of 1944 was a genuine *taking of power* by the people in Limoges, Valence, Toulouse, the Alps, to a much greater extent than in the north of France where the political game was played from the top down.

Since May '68, this shift has been accentuated. Rome is no longer the hub of the universe. Paris is no longer the centre of France. The Parisians have learned to step down from their pedestal and go out to the rest of the country rather than wait for the provinces to 'come up' to them. That pretty little word, 'province', derives — incidentally — from *pro-vincere*, meaning the assumption of responsibility for the defeated. Such is the geopolitics of the new working-class struggles that are uninhibited by the traditional 'respect for the tools of work' and passive obedience to union 'delegates' enjoying the exclusive right to negotiate with employers. It is in the west of France that some of the most advanced struggles have recently taken place, with sequestration of the managers, active coopera-tion with the radical peasants of the area and occasionally the assumption by the workers of responsibility for production; the main points of con-flict have been Saint-Nazaire, the bitter industrial conflict at the *Joint Français* electric plant at Saint-Brieuc, Fougères, Cerisay. These are newly industrialized areas, relatively unaffected by traditional trade unionism and its reflexes; the working class there includes a large proportion of 'undis-ciplined' workers — uprooted peasants, youths, immigrants, women, all of whom have no ingrained 'respect for the tools of work.' Already in May '68 there was a visible geopolitical discrepancy with respect to strike militancy in the various Renault plants around the country; it was *inversely* proportional to the 'experience' and trade-union 'background' of the workers in each plant. The strike broke out at Cléon in Normandy almost in the middle of the fields, then spread to Flins in the Ile-de-France; the last to join the movement was the Renault 'stronghold' at Billancourt just outside Paris, where the 'experienced cadres' of the C.G.T. were finally forced to act.

But while the decentralization of people's struggles is a reality in France, the fact remains that each one unfolds in isolation, without reference to what is happening elsewhere, or to the situation as a whole. Can there be such a thing as a unified, anti-centralist strategy?

18 Breaking the shell of history: the interdisciplinary approach

Expand the list of history's auxiliary disciplines, or challenge the auto-nomy of history with respect to other social sciences? – an inter-disciplinary approach for the university world or for the movement? – ethnohistory or active solidarity with the peoples of the Third World? – the Vietnam war and an 'underground' interdisciplinary approach

Professional conformism has its limits. Academic historians are increasingly interested in the idea of an 'interdisciplinary' approach and now claim that they would like to do away with the barriers separating history from other disciplines. In some cases, it is merely a matter of keeping up-to-date with the latest intellectual fashions and expanding somewhat their repertoire of 'attractive' themes and subjects of research. For the interdisciplinary approach opens up a whole new field of activity to the knowledge-power system on which the entire little world of academic historians is based. The more ingenious among them will manage to identify the links and bridges capable of connecting fields of study that nobody ever dreamed of bringing together before. All that is needed is to master quickly a new technical vocabulary and read a few well-chosen works in a field previously unfamiliar to most historians – and *presto*, one more 'brilliant career' is spectacularly launched: historical ethnomusicology, economic anthropology or the semiotic analysis of historical documents, to take a few examples.

Others feel sincerely that history really needs new fields to conquer, new perspectives to open up, new insights to acquire from other social sciences: economics, linguistics, sociology, psychoanalysis, etc. But the resulting enrichment, rather than bringing into question the rules and conventions of the academic historians' rhetoric, merely gives it new substance and authority. The interdisciplinary approach may even facilitate the historian's attempt to extend his influence over all the human sciences from the central position that many claim for themselves as legitimate proprietors of the entire time dimension.

There are still others who view the impossible interdisciplinary quest as a disturbing critique of historical science itself as an 'established' discipline. Within the university world, then, the interdisciplinary approach has three different meanings:

■ *Expanding the list of history's 'auxiliary sciences'.* Although the historians, of course, avoid putting it in such terms so as to avoid wounding the vanity of their 'colleagues' in other disciplines, whose co-operation is indispensable to the success of this patchwork operation. The sciences traditionally considered as auxiliary to history are those concerned with the techniques required for the handling and processing of historical materials: diplomatics and palaeography for the Middle Ages, epigraphy and numismatics for antiquity, archival science for modern history. The list now includes *linguistics* –taking inventory of the stock of words relating to a particular moment of history, the study of the language-structure characteristic of a given period. *Mathematics* and *computers* are indispensable tools for the 'treatment' of the quantified material which is a must for the historian's prestige and for formalistic abstractions in the cliometrics style. *Social psychology* and *psychoanalysis* add substantially to the historian's intellectual equipment and enable him to cope more effectively with problems of collective consciousness and mass mentality. The list could be extended further.

These new contributions are neither good nor bad in themselves. All deepen the historian's insight into the objective reality of phenomena. There is, for example, a typically Stalinist 'rhetoric' with its own syntax and rhythm; the techniques of linguistics can help us grasp the political phenomenon of Stalinism. *Psychoanalysis* enables us to identify deeper impulses and collective non-verbalized states of mind, to decipher apparently innocent or insignificant behaviour patterns. But these new tools are worth no more than historical science itself. In no way do they alter its basic social role, its isolation. They can improve the quality of the historian's answers only if the questions are raised in quite a different spirit.

The same can be said of the natural sciences recently mobilized in the service of archaeology, or the chronological study of 'societies with-out history'. The resources here are immense, as is the danger of becom-ing hypnotized by the new gadgetry of those 'auxiliary sciences': dendro-chronology (dating by the annual rings around tree trunks); Carbon 14 (measuring the radioactivity of ancient metals that decreases with their age); the stratigraphy of soils (alluvial river deposits, glacial deposits, wind deposits); archaeomagnetism (long-term variations of magnetism); coprolithology (the study of fossilized excrement, its age, composition and location); the analysis of fossilized pollens; palaeo-ethnobotany (the study of the plants cultivated in prehistoric societies); palaeopathology (the science of diseases detected in ancient human remains, particularly in graves); spectroscopy of fossilized metals to identify alloys known to primitive metallurgy; submarine archaeology; archaeology by aerial photography, etc. The list is long and particularly attractive for social science specialists anxious to 'get close to reality' and to appear as rigorous and as well-equipped as their scientific colleagues. And besides, the purely intellectual appeal of these new 'auxiliary sciences' is multiplied by more tangible advantages, such as a taste of outdoors life and a chance to manipulate complex equipment, which brighten up and enliven the rather dull and spartan existence of the average social scientist.

Here again, the criticism concerns not the techniques themselves but the use to which they are put: either the meticulous accumulation of information sought as an end in itself – and which serves, incidentally, as a source of prestige and personal advantage; or a better *active* understanding of a past that, while far removed in time, still has a meaning for us and speaks to our present concerns. Archaeology can certainly serve political ends. The neolithic village of Panpo, near Zhengzhou, completely unearthed by careful excavation, receives thousands of visitors daily. The guides and posters emphasize the uninterrupted efforts of the Chinese peasantry throughout the ages, the historical succession of social systems, the sexist distribution of social roles that prevailed in those faraway epochs.

■ *The juxtaposition of distinct disciplines for the purpose of studying a concrete phenomenon.* This interdisciplinary practice is particularly well adapted to the mechanisms of the university bureaucracy. Each specialist continues to function in terms of his own rhetoric – geographical, historical, economic, linguistic, etc. – and the results are stuck together end to end. Under such conditions, funds are more easily obtained, whether the subject of the research is Nepal or a Breton village like Plozevec that was thrown open around 1960 to the combined onslaught of teams of linguists, historians, sociologists, ethnologists – each team working, in the last analysis, on its own. The results were inevitably disappointing. In such a case, the interdisciplinary approach is little more than an attractive advertising slogan.

■ *A basic rethinking of the relationship between historical science and another discipline* (for example, economics, or anthropology, or sociology). Carried out in a consistent and radical way, this deep-going interdisciplinary approach can lead to a critique of the separation of studies and the present division of labour among the social sciences. The science of economic phenomena, for example, could certainly benefit from an historical dimension, as could the science of social organization. For in the course of time, the phenomena they study have varied considerably, not only in their details but in their basic nature. Yet as the other social sciences acquire a historical dimension – and this implies a reciprocal process of breaking down the traditional barriers of separation – the specific function of historical science itself will have to be radically reconsidered. When certain historians propose, in all sincerity, a basic pooling of efforts in the fields of economic history and theoretical economics, are they merely trying to enrich conventional historical rhetoric by the development of better theoretical tools? Or are they actually willing to see historical science itself eventually absorbed in the global study of human societies?

This question can hardly be answered so long as we remain confined within the university world. Perhaps the whole problem of the interdisciplinary approach is, after all, a false one. Clever reformers have come up with no lack of gimmicks: interdisciplinary seminars, preferably held in an ancient abbey; long-range research projects, preferably in distant places; whole battalions of helpers to do the dirty work; entire batteries of computers; 'epistemological' exploration by an intellectual pioneer who has mastered two or more disciplines. But all that amounts to little more than a few new technical formulae for either veterans or novices in the field. It remains within the limits of the academic establishment and merely revitalizes its essential values: intellectualism, professionalism, productivism. It is no accident that the members or ex-members of the student and teacher trade-unions, accustomed to assuming responsibility for managing the affairs of the university, feel particularly at ease with this attempt to remodel the out-dated structures of the academic world in line with the new interdisciplinary approach.

There have also been some serious recent efforts to do away with the traditional separation between history and anthropology. By way of answer to the lifeless structuralist approach, it was not irrelevant to demonstrate that the 'societies without a history' (so called because they left no written records) also have their time-dimension, that their past can be known through their own oral traditions, through the reports of foreign travellers, or through such specialized modern techniques as stratigraphy and dendrochronology. These people, moreover, are aware of their own past. The Cherokees, for example, know that their nation, with its specific characteristics, took shape through an *historical process* and made its home two thousand years ago in the Little Tennessee area. All this belongs to what is called enthnohistory or historical ethnology. At the same time, we of the West should not forget that there is no qualitative difference between the non-Western 'primitive' societies and the ancient historical societies from which we ourselves have sprung. The ancient Greeks, the Celts, the Teutons – all were 'savages' in the ethnographer's sense of the word.

What purpose is served by recapturing the historical dimension of these stateless societies of the past and present? Are these peoples merely the passive object of debate among Western intellectuals; or have they a role of their own to play? Raising the question in this way means recognizing that the problems of ethnohistory are more than an intellectual pastime — a more fascinating one, it is true, than the sterile, static mathematics of structuralist anthropology. The question focuses attention on the *future* of these peoples. It reverses the past-present relationship. To say that no people can be excluded from history is a way of saying that every people has a right to a future of its own, a future that is not defined from the outside by others in terms of such conceptual traps as 'underdevelopment' or 'acculturation' that are loaded with economic and cultural imperialism. To define this future, each people not only has a right to a past of its own, but also needs such a past. Who is to exercise that right or proclaim that need, whether in the past or in the future? Will it be the anthropologist, perhaps one converted to ethnohistory like Robert Jaulin, for example, who is waging a courageous fight against ethnocide in Amazonia? Or the peoples concerned? Or a combination of the two? Once again, the problem is to define the link between the knowledge of the intellectual — even one with the best of intentions — and mass struggles. Unless this problem is tackled, the interdisciplinary approach remains little more than a parlour game for curriculum-makers and the technocrats of scientific research.

The real impulse for interdisciplinary federalism is to be found outside the university world. Once again, we return to social practice, and with it comes the unifying theoretical deliberation which derives from practice and provides it with substance and coherence. Those who have had the experience of putting together an information kit for use by immigrant workers in their struggles or for a campaign against the World Bank, or for militant Occitania theatre groups, will recognize the necessity of the interdisciplinary approach. For such purposes, they must inevitably join with others in a collective effort to assemble facts, documents, ideas from such varied fields as history, economics, social psychology, linguistics, medical sociology. And it is out of the question to go about it by merely juxtaposing, sticking together, separate pieces of information borrowed from linguists, historians, economists. In most cases, the partial knowledge of the various specialists fails to provide the answers to the questions that are being raised. Social practice awakens new curiosities, revealing the inadequacy of academic knowledge. Aroused people have to look for the answers on their own.

The American militants involved in the struggle against the war in Vietnam learned this through experience in their campaign against the giant Minneapolis firm, Honeywell, which took part in the production of anti-personnel bombs. Their intention was to denounce this powerful multinational corporation as a war criminal and demonstrate its responsibility for genocide in Vietnam. But the enormous mass of material put out year after year by the economics departments of the American universities was of almost no use to them. All such highly specialized studies were far too respectful of the administrative rules and regulations, the financial tricks and political secrets that protect the big multinational companies from public scrutiny. On the pretext of remaining strictly technical, those academic studies deliberately avoid any examination of key problems like the nature of the social and political groups that control the powerful corporations, their ideology, their collusion with the military, their quasi-governmental political role. The answers to these questions had to be sought through 'underground' research carried out by inexperienced, unpaid militants digging diligently through the 'Who's Who' of the business world. Research organizations independent of the universities have played a vital role in the denunciation of the Vietnam war and other ventures of American imperialism – NARMIC, for example, with its research on the military-industrial complex; NACLA which concentrates on Latin America; the SESPA, which consists of scientists and engineers committed to political action.*

The 'interdisciplinary approach' had become a requirement of the struggle in the United States rather than an end in itself.

To enable history to break out of its academic shell, it becomes necessary once again to challenge the privileged and yet miserably narrow role of the intellectual who looks out timidly upon the world from behind his window and – for amusement – dreamily traces fly-legs on the morning frost, as Lu Xun put it.

*NARMIC = National Action Research on the Military Industrial Complex (sponsored by the U.S. Society of Friends); NACLA = North American Council on Latin America; SESPA = Scientists and Engineers for Social and Political Action.

19 In search of a history for the revolution

What kind of 'histoire immédiate'? − what kind of technical division of historical labour? at whose request? − 'theoretical practice': a frog at the bottom of its well − the mass demand for history and the collective memory − traps in the 'cult of the revolutionary past': ritual anniversaries, historic leaders and strategic blueprints − the past as revolutionary ferment; what current struggles owe to their anchoring in history − examples, not models − the spectre of Zhdanovism exorcized by Gramsci's 'organic intellectuals' − a general historical summing-up, istoricismo assoluto, which spells the end of history as a specialized discipline

A debate has been under way among French historians on the question of 'histoire immédiate' − the study of 'history in the making'. Conventional history is increasingly uncomfortable as it approaches the present; a certain 'distance' is supposedly needed, since a stance of 'objectivity' is not easy to maintain when dealing with 'burning' issues. The secrecy of the archives, a typical form of the power of the ruling class over history, is invoked in this connection not only as an evasion but also as an intellectual requirement: a thirty years' wait for State secrets, fifty years for family histories, a hundred for Vatican affairs.

By way of reaction, there are those who, hoping to extend the scope of history by dealing with subjects familiar to the general public, stress the advantages of 'histoire immédiate': the variety and abundance of available documents; the use of oral testimony, eye-witness accounts and opinion polls; the smooth cooperation with other social scientists such as sociologists, demographers, political scientists whose basic data consist almost entirely of contemporary materials; the historian's close familiarity with his subject through personal experience. Agreed! In comparison with the apologists of conventional history and its canons, the increasingly numerous partisans of 'histoire immédiate' have the better of the argument.

Although 'histoire immédiate' provides a genuine opening to the realities of today's world, in no way does it modify the usual rules of the history Establishment. The past it deals with, while very recent, is still outside ourselves. When a panel of distinguished university professors analyze the domestic and international developments of the past year on a Christmas television programme, all they do is move the machine for cutting and wrapping up history as close as possible to ourselves; but that machine functions in exactly the same old way. Our ability to think historically about the present is not strengthened but weakened by these performances of 'histoire immédiate', since even the most recent past is caught in the jaws of the history machine.

At the same time, 'histoire immédiate' is one of the more attractive forms of history-as-merchandise. 'Mere journalism,' say the conventional academics. The fact is that these books of 'histoire immédiate' make history 'come alive' with more talent and success than many a more scholarly work. But while they are close to the people in their language and their familiarity with the news, they remain distant in most essential respects. Their work is not based on the people's real day-to-day concerns, and all they try to do is entertain or 'inform'.

The function of 'histoire immédiate' should, on the contrary, be to link the open-ended present, with all its potentialities, to the recent past. For what matters is not the techniques and methods used, the polls and surveys, the mountains of press clippings, the eagerly-collected pamphlets and documents. The main point, once again, is to base the work on the demands of social practice and of the political struggle. The researchers of the O.R.S.T.O.M. (*Office de la recherche scientifique et technique d'outremer*,* with headquarters in Paris) may go into the villages of Madagascar to do a study on the nationalist rebellion of 1947 with an elaborate questionnaire, the most modern tape-recorders, the 'best trained' assistants. All they will be able to do is accumulate disconnected items of information without internal consistency. Only a Madagascar revolutionary movement and those connected with it — because they are driven by a need to understand the political and social realities of their island in order to develop a political strategy — are capable of grasping the historical significance and real nature of the 1947 revolt, its causes and the meaning of its failure. For a revolutionary movement definitely requires such an analysis, assuming it is prepared to examine the facts with the utmost rigour rather than being satisfied with facile mythical images.

Such an analysis would undoubtedly involve technical research methods, oral surveys, recourse to eye-witness survivors of the rebellion, archival research, an examination of press and propaganda materials which are not always easily obtainable. But these research techniques are justified only in the context of an overall political project. The technical division of

* Office of overseas scientific and technical research.

labour and the use of the historian's specialized know-how can be very precious, *on condition that such a division of labour be collectively determined by all concerned rather than claimed as a right by historians alone.* We must be willing to participate in a collective effort to think historically about the present and to think politically about the past — in a responsible way, of course, but never from a position of professional privilege in the name of our special 'knowledge'. It is not for us to choose 'freely' our specific role in the field of history. We must be prepared to have the demand come from elsewhere. Elsewhere? In this society of class and privilege, the *social demand* will in most cases be addressed to historians by organized groups or political militants rather than by the masses. The dehumanizing machine has been in operation for centuries and the road to complete grass-roots democracy is long and tortuous. Whether we like it or not, we shall have to accept the fact that the struggle will usually be waged under the direction of the most active elements.

The idea that the demand for history should come from outside the profession is not to the liking of the 'Marxist historians' comfortably installed in the juxtaposed bureaucracies of the university and the Communist Party. They are sincerely convinced that Marxism is an instrument for the analysis of society enabling those who have mastered it to attain something like scientific accuracy. But their aim is limited to promoting 'historical research' based on Marxist principles, for they accept the ground-rules or bourgeois academic history: specialization, technicism, productivism, hierarchy. They draw a line of separation between Marxism's capacity to interpret society, including the past, scientifically, and its basic goal — to change the world. In doing so, they also separate theory from practice in defiance of the Marxist principle that their unity is indispensable to scientific knowledge. Academic Marxist historians confuse the potential *capacity* of Marxism to provide a scientific analysis of any area of history, any past society, with the concrete and *preferential* application of Marxism to the study of just *those* historical phenomena that can shed light on today's struggles. Like other academic historians, they feel free to choose the speciality that appeals to them personally. In any case, they think, such work can only increase the intellectual influence of Marxism in the university world; the prestige they acquire will serve the cause of the working class and the revolution. Intellectual activity becomes a political end in itself.

Pierre Vilar, a leading French Marxist historian, has on several occasions defined quite frankly this choice, this division of labour between professional historians of the Marxist obedience and political cadres. Only 'geniuses', like Marx, Engels, Mao, he says, are able to establish a direct link between theory and practice, to integrate an analysis of the past and reflection about the past with the elaboration of a political strategy. So far as the average historian is concerned, it is enough for him to fulfil his 'civic duties' — to vote, perhaps even to 'militate'; but without letting his political views interfere with his personal research. He is happy to be a humble day-labourer of specialized historical research along Marxist lines. To integrate the results of his research with constant political reflection is the task of a centralized General Staff in which the individual Communist historian is expected to place his confidence. And in any case, the founders of Marxism have supposedly done the basic work; the theoretical and political 'tool' of Marxism exists ready-made and all that remains is to master its use. And yet the theory-practice link — in this case, the link between historical research and political thinking — is in reality a continuous creation that should be carried out at the base no less than at the summit and in connection with day-to-day struggles no less than with long-term strategy.

The 'theoretical practice' dear to the heart of Althusser and his followers is little more than a somewhat better codified, more explicit, more openly élitist, form of the conceptions and practices widespread in the French Communist Party. The 'social practice' of intellectuals is expected to take the form of autonomous theoretical reflection — discussion with other intellectuals somewhere in the university neighbour-hood of the Latin Quarter is regarded as a kind of 'practice'. The intellec-tual, the historian, can *think* for himself on the basis of exchanges with other intellectuals or the reading of papers. Personal participation in on-going working-class struggles is not considered necessary to creative theoretical work. The intellectual's historical understanding can develop far from the scene of political action.

This brings us back again to the old question of the relationship be-tween form and content. For the academic Marxist, the content (in other words, his own rhetoric) counts much more than the form — the inescapable compromises with Establishment institutions. And yet it would seem that the reverse is true. The reality, after all, is social prac-tice, the relationship among people both in the special field of history and in society as a whole, which is influenced by historical knowledge and the élitist circumstances of its development. That is the *content*. The rhetoric — even if Marxist in its terms — is secondary so long as it functions in isolation, within the framework of an élitist academic practice. It is, in the last analysis, only the *form*.

We must be extremely demanding. The study of the past and histori-cal reflection must be linked to mass struggles and a revolutionary strategy. And for that, we have to leave the university ghetto of academic historians. We have to listen to the workers, their experience, their questions. There is a Chinese proverb that Mao liked to repeat: For the frog fallen to the bottom of the well, the sky is no wider than the opening at the top of the

well. The well, in this case, might be the new Jussieu campus of Paris
University, or some other such spot.

One fact is undeniable: the existence of a mass demand for history.
The success of history-as-merchandise in all its forms is only the expression, taken over and perverted by the consumer society, of a genuine
popular demand. I have already referred to Claude Manceron's remark
that there is 'a deep hunger for history among the people.' The French
press has recently publicized the success of the amateur 'genealogy clubs'.
Who are we? What are our origins? It is interesting to know, for example,
that one's ancestors were small farmers of the Ile de France, or fishermen
on the Niger river, or kosher butchers on the Lower East Side of New York.
The numerous, moving letters received by S. Moatti, producer of the recent
television film entitled *Pain Noir* about the life of French peasants and
workers, often came from simple people who recognized themselves and
their problems in the show — particularly in the scenes about peasants
driven from the land by impoverishment, workers on strike facing the
rifles of the police, the discovery of the sea with the first two-week paid
vacations won under the Popular Front, the anti-Nazi underground, etc.

E. H. Carr, in *What is History*, wrote:

> One reason why history rarely repeats itself among historically-
> conscious people is that the dramatis personae are aware, at the
> second performance, of the *denouement* of the first, and their action
> is affected by that knowledge. The Bolsheviks knew that the French
> revolution had ended in a Napoleon, and feared that their own revo-
> lution might end in the same way. They therefore mistrusted Trotsky,
> who among the leaders looked most like a Napoleon, and trusted
> Stalin, who looked least like a Napoleon.

But the collective memory is not neutral. At times, it can play a
negative role, acting as a trap, a lure. The desire to reproduce the past
artificially is not confined to reactionaries, and examples abound of
the 'cult of the revolutionary past'. In 1848, the revolutionaries of Paris
reopened the Jacobin club that had flourished in 1789, and in 1871 they
produced a newspaper called *Le Père Duchesne*, named for the journal of
Hébert that was so influential during the first French Revolution. Jean
Bruhat clearly analyzed what he describes as the French labour movement's tendency toward 'historical mimicry' as exemplified by such
slogans as: 'Carry out the mission of 1789!' 'Execute the testament of
Jacobinism!' But he refrains, of course, from defining the class bases
and the ideological content of this phenomenon: the contamination of
the French proletariat by petit-bourgeois thinking. Marx, who was free
of national prejudice and chauvinism, put it more sharply in September
1870 after the proclamation of the Third Republic: 'The tragedy of the

French, as well as of the workers, lies in their *big memories*. Events must put an end once and for all to this *reactionary cult of the past*.'*

That 'reactionary cult of the past' is still rife today. How often do we hear talk in the French labour movement of 'another '36'! In May '68, the leaders of the CGT, France's largest trade-union federation, naively tried to play for a second time the scenario of June '36, with the same leading actor of national stature, Benoît Frachon, the same prestigious stage — the vast Billancourt square facing the Renault plant — and the same élite public, the workers of the largest factory of France. But this time the audience booed! The strikers of May '68 refused to give the union leaders a blank check to negotiate behind their backs. Georges Séguy, General Secretary of the CGT, had to return for further discussions. Meanwhile, back in the heart of Paris, the same cult of the past was raging among the students of that 'beautiful May' with their utopian slogans à la Fourier, their barricades in the style of 1832 or 1848, their revolutionary populism whose lyricism failed to conceal their isolation within the restricted area of the Latin Quarter.

The revolutionary reference to a venerated past is often, as in the Renault case, a useful technique for channelling mass struggles, reducing them to 'tried and tested' models in order to stifle creativity. In 1931, the Maoist peasant strategy — based on armed struggle, the seizure of power in limited areas, the long range view — was a new departure with respect to the Bolshevik model of 1917: win or lose all in a few decisive days. Yet the Stalinist majority in the leadership of the Chinese Communist Party (the 'twenty-eight Bolsheviks' back from Moscow) managed to impose the label of 'Chinese soviets' on these original political creations. They wanted to give the impression of conforming to the orthodox model. They carried their concern for detail so far as to choose 7 November as the day on which to proclaim the birth of the Republic of Chinese Soviets in the Red zones.

Gramsci was acutely sensitive to the limiting, weakening influence of these references to the past and to the models of the past. For him, the October Revolution was a revolution 'against *Das Kapital*', a revolution that defied the rules of the game and refused to conform to the oversimplified scheme of the theoreticians of the Second International, for whom the basic message of Marx's famous book was the inevitability of socialist revolutions in the most advanced industrialized countries:

> The facts have exploded the critical schemes within which the history of Russia was supposed to unfold, according to the canons of historical materialism. The Bolsheviks repudiate Karl Marx when they declare that, in the light of their own achievements and victories, the canons

* Letter from Marx to César de Paepe, 14 September 1870.

of historical materialism are not so rigid as people might think and
did think. . . .

But while the Bolsheviks reject certain statements in *Capital*, they
do not reject the invigorating thought that permeates it. They are
simply not 'Marxists'. They have not compiled, on the basis of the
Master's works, an external body of doctrine consisting of dogmatic
assertions that are considered beyond discussion. They live Marxist
thought − that which will never die − . . . and this thought recognizes
as the vital factor of history not raw economic phenomena but man
and human society . . .*

The concept of the 'historic leader' in revolutionary movements plays
the same negative role as models. The reader has already seen to what
extent the action of individuals in history is typically ephemeral and
discontinuous. But there are individuals who are tempted to survive their
day of glory by clinging to their past and to the image that events have
engraved in the popular mind. They play on their fame and prestige,
stifle the creativity of the people, intimidate the young militants, throw
their weight around a little too much. In the national and social liberation
movements of the Third World, this phenomenon of the 'historic leader'
causes at least as much damage as in the people's movements of the West;
Bourguiba and Haile Selassie, Tchang Kai-chek and Gandhi, Messali and
Soekarno are examples. Few are wise enough to smash their own statues
as Sihanouk did. Was Mao another such 'historic leader'? The idealized
image of the 'Great Helmsman' with his rich experience was popularized
by Lin Piao during the Cultural Revolution, and Mao was apparently
resigned to it, at least temporarily. But, on the other hand, Mao assumed
the risk, during that same Cultural Revolution, of opening up a period
of disorder that he considered necessary for purposes of political clarification and mass mobilization. To this imperative, he sacrificed the
solidity of the very power which his own historic status had conferred
on him.

The 'historic leader' is often a kind of 'exalted father' character whose
primary political role consists of 'protecting' the people long after his
death; before him, they kneel respectfully, passively. Lenin's corpse lies
in a mausoleum in Moscow, Ho Chi Minh's lies in Hanoi and Mao's in
Peking − but Karl Marx is buried inconspicuously in London.

Historical rhetoric represents a trap in still another sense − it puts
forward *sequential* models of successive strategic stages: the national-
democratic revolution, the seizure of power, the transitional phase, the
passage to socialism, the revolutionary attack against the superstructures −
such is the Chinese pattern. Or the defensive war of movement, the
balance of forces, the victorious counter-offensive − such was the Viet-

---

* A. Gramsci, *Ecrits politiques*, v. I, Paris 1975.

namese military pattern of the First Indochina War (1946—54). But
these patterns are so many brakes. In Vietnam, for example, the war
against the United States in the south did not go through the same stages
as the war against France in the north. Madagascar will not repeat the
same revolutionary stages as did the Chinese Revolution, and Argentina
will not follow precisely in the footsteps of the Cuban revolution.

Should the existence of all these historical traps lead us to the con-
clusion that 'forgetfulness is bliss', a fashionable attitude these days
among the French neo-Nietzscheans? No — for such intellectual acro-
batics neglect a basic fact: the past is both an anchor and a trap because
it is *primarily a right*. It is not for a few intellectuals or militant minorities to pick and choose from the past — without reference to the common sense of the people or their collective thinking — in an attempt to
devise historical models, historical symbols or historic leaders. The right
to a collective memory means the right to define which aspects of past
experience count the most and are of greatest help. 'Away with all the
old traditions!' Yes — if it means sweeping away all the traps of historical
models and references. But why not use the past both to serve the present
and to open the way to the future?

In China, conventional historical rhetoric has not yet been discarded.
Tourists are frequently treated — as I know from experience — to interminable lectures on some episode of Party history or the details concerning the administrative changes that took place when a coalmine was trans-
ferred from its former British owners. Here, as in many other areas, the
'struggle between two lines' is a reality. In China the mobilizing force
of historic reference-points in popular experience is a recognized fact.
The 'May 7 Schools' are defined by a date that expresses more than a
political slogan, for it consecrates the gains of the Cultural Revolution.
And in the museums, works of art are not simply 'put on display' — i.e.,
exhibited for their own sake, for purely aesthetic purposes — but placed
in their historical and social context as the products both of technical
knowledge and of an oppressive social order. Workers are encouraged
to write the 'four histories'. The relationship to the past acts as a revolutionary ferment.

In France, too, the past can play the role of revolutionary ferment.
Many examples of such anchoring have been mentioned in these pages.
In the countryside today, the radical 'peasant-worker' movement tries
to detect, by appealing to the people's collective memory, the local cases
of polarization of wealth: the enrichment of certain families and the impoverishment of others in the space of a mere two or three generations.
These are so many concrete signs, easily perceptible to the people of the
economic mechanisms operating in twentieth-century French society.
The grandfather who engaged in black-marketeering under the Nazi

Occupation and the one who had to sell his land because he couldn't make ends meet, are facts one does not forget, however painful it may be to talk about them.

Dario Fo, the Italian revolutionary militant, has clearly demonstrated, with his street theatre, how the past can be used to provide ammunition for the people's struggles. He has reached back to the medieval jongleurs seemingly so far removed from the realities of contemporary capitalism, and has revived their subversive qualities to denounce the rich and bring out the cultural creativity of the people as a way of bolstering their confidence in their capacity for political action.

> The aim of this artistic mixture of various medieval texts that Comrade Fo assembled from all over Europe during many years of research is less the philological rediscovery of literary and theatrical forms of expression than their reinterpretation with a view to recapturing the full range of their authentic values − especially their power as a force of critical opposition to an overwhelmingly oppressive society and their militant affirmation of an alternative to the values of the ruling class.
>
> The grotesque humour so characteristic of the street jongleurs has always been a weapon of critical satire against the Establishment. A universal weapon of all periods and all peoples. That is why Dario Fo's message in his rendition of *Mistero Buffo* − whether through his reinvention of ancient texts, preserving intact their original vigour, or through the presentation of such texts in a politically stimulating way − is not of merely historical interest; his object is to rewrite the history of the mass culture of the exploited from their own standpoint, and not from that of the ruling class, on the premise that only a knowledge of the past experience of the people, the moving force of history, can provide genuine clues for action today in the struggle for socialist liberation.*

Examples of anchoring in the past, such as China, Dario Fo, the peasant memory, or the Irish political arena, are in no sense an inventory of models to be copied mechanically. They are mentioned here to emphasize the overwhelming necessity of *concrete inventiveness*. 'Self-criticism' is fashionable among left-wing intellectuals. Many feel a *malaise* and would undoubtedly agree with most of the objections to conventional history expressed in this book. But objections and criticism are not enough. What new means of expression can we develop for historical research and historical knowledge? Grass-roots surveys? Political theatre? Comic strips? And what kind of books shall we write − assuming any are needed? What teaching methods should be used? By reaction against the passive, ivory tower tone of conventional historical rhetoric − the famous academic 'detachment', meaning detachment from any form of political commitment − the emphasis here has been on a living link between historical

---

* From a leaflet distributed on the occasion of Dario Fo's visit to Paris in 1973.

knowledge and social practice. But such links cannot be created in a vacuum. They require a minimum of background knowledge − a kind of 'primitive accumulation', to borrow the language of the historians of seventeenth-century capitalism. How are we to define this basic stock of indispensable knowledge? How is it to be built up − through textbooks, encyclopaedias? How will they be made available to the general public?

Is integrating historical knowledge with social practice − in terms of the concrete demands of ongoing mass struggles − a return to Zhdanovism, whose ill-cleansed corpse still infects the thinking of so many people, and not only those who were once influenced by the Communist Parties of the West in the 1950s? Is it a return to the mechanical dichotomy between 'bourgeois' history and 'proletarian' history? That thesis, formulated in 1952 by Zhdanov and Stalin − and immediately embraced by all the Communist Parties − had its hour of glory and provoked many a political crisis and personal tragedy. It was quickly abandoned after Stalin's death in favour of a scientific liberalism that co-exists smoothly with the institutions of the bourgeois university. Is history devoid of class character? Very well, then − Marxist historians, get to work on your doctoral theses!

This new 'line' had the merit of simplicity and convenience. But it evaded a problem that is now recognized as vital: what type of social relationships are *produced* by a given science, whether bourgeois or proletarian. By what kind of social practice is it characterized? From this standpoint, is there really much difference between the intellectual terrorism of the Zhdanov period and anti-Zhdanovist liberalism? In both cases, a science is defined as the intellectual product of individual brains functioning in splendid isolation. There are, of course, conflicting views about the status of science, which the 'liberals' regard as independent of class relationships, while, in the Zhdanovist view, it is defined as a product of either the bourgeoisie or the proletariat. But in both cases, it is a body of knowledge that develops intellectually without any real connection with the social practice of the intellectuals themselves.

When I suggest that in the West today historical knowledge is an integral part of capitalist ideology and of bourgeois social relations, this does not represent a return to Zhdanovism. For all Zhdanov proposed in reality was the mechanical transference of the intellectual's allegiance from the bourgeoisie to the proletariat. He never once questioned the role of élitist knowledge in society; and Soviet 'socialist' science was no less academic at the time of Zhdanov than at the time of Brezhnev. 'Academic' is used here to mean cut off from the mass of people and without any *genuine* political initiative and responsibility. Today, our break with bourgeois historical science is being carried out from a quite different *critical* perspective. It owes far more to Gramsci than to the

official Communist apparatus: the conventional intellectuals are agents
of the ruling ideology and belong to the 'old historic bloc'; but they
enjoy a certain margin of initiative — it is their responsibility to break
with the old ideology, join the 'new historic bloc' and become 'organic
intellectuals'. What radically separates the Zhdanovist *apparatchnik* of
the 1950s from Gramsci's 'organic intellectual' is, in the last analysis,
the idea that *in the West socialism has yet to be invented*. And the intellectuals have their place in that common search, without negating themselves but renouncing their privileged status.

In the 1950s, Marxist intellectuals, particularly historians, could
choose between only two attitudes: either yield to the propaganda and
pressures urging them to break with bourgeois historical science in favour
of an even more rigid form of historical science, or fall back upon
academic liberalism with a sigh of 'cowardly relief' as we all did at the
time, and thereby *renounce all political criticism* of the history
Establishment. The 'free-lancers' capable of rejecting these alternatives
were few and far between. Today we are in a position to be both more
demanding and more modest. Our role is to try to integrate ourselves
'organically' with the people's struggles so that — through such struggles
and together with all who are exploited — we may participate in the task
of inventing socialism in the West on the basis of Marxism.

As suggested in Chapter I, history as an academic discipline is only a
limited version of the 'collective relationship to the past'. This collective
relationship is, in turn, only one aspect of a more general relationship:
*man's insertion into the time-dimension, and his awareness of this inser-
tion.* The past matters only in relation to the future; history's function
is to open up the future.

It is the entire past that must be grasped, taking as the point of departure the political objectives and strategic options of the present. Brecht
once said that the most obnoxious feature of a bureaucracy is its memory.
Gramsci urged us to 'take possession of our own memory as the product
of an historical process which developed to this point and has left in us
an infinity of traces — we have only to take stock of them.' That is why
Gramsci defined Marxism as an *istoricismo assoluto* — an exploration of
the past without omission, restriction or fear. Mao adopts a similar
approach when he defines the basic function of history as that of summing up human experience, 'discovering, inventing, creating and advancing'
to enable mankind to develop 'from the realm of necessity to that of
freedom.'

But who is to identify the 'links of the chain' (Gramsci) or do the
'summing up' (Mao)? In other words, what kind of history can be of use
to the Revolution? Just as we 'professional' historians cannot claim the
exclusive right to establish in detail the technical division of historical

labour with respect to the concrete requirements of the struggle, neither have we the authority to carry out, exactly as we please, the indispensable task of theoretical synthesis concerning the interrelationship between the past and the future. If we seek comfort in the seclusion of our own minds and our own books we shall be disqualified from participation in the common effort of research and invention. We must reject the role of privileged dispensers of knowledge; the fact is that we are no more enthusiastic about such a role than are other social science 'specialists', such as the anthropologists.

> The same old story! Change society — agreed! Change the role of the intellectual — agreed! But let us all remain students and researchers — agreed again! Let others saw down the tree — we shall stay seated on our branch!*

How can the past prepare the future? General reflection on the past, historical thinking in the best sense of the word, can be coherent and fruitful only if based on a consistent analysis of the present. Its existence is justified only if it is integrated into a theoretically elaborated revolutionary strategy. Historians can, of course, participate fully in such an effort, but certainly not on their own. In this sense, we must be willing to have our 'territory' expropriated — and participate thereafter in the common effort of historical thinking only at the call of the community and in cooperation with it. But how will such a demand be formulated — and by whom? How can the professionals be expropriated? How can historical knowledge be socialized without giving up the demand for scientific accuracy? These questions are both urgent and inescapable but they cannot be answered by intellectuals alone. 'At the beginning of the world,' said Lu Xun, 'there were no roads on the earth; as men walked — one behind the other — roads were traced.'

Must we, then, 'finish history off'? The answer is 'Yes!' if by history is meant an elitist, specialized, academic discipline — an ideological rhetoric putting the past in command, in the interest of the power structure and the ruling class. In that sense, Marx wanted to 'finish off philosophy' as we would speak of 'finishing off' a scourge or an illusion. Today, historians are not the only ones to reflect on the disappearance pure and simple of their particular discipline.

'To think about and desire the end of anthropology as a specialized field of knowledge, cut off from the social groups that "reproduce" it indirectly, from *those who are its subject.*' Again it is the anthropologist, J. Copans (*op. cit.*), speaking.

But how can we 'finish history' in the way that we might finish a house, a trip, a harvest? 'Let us make a clean slate of the past!' That

---

* J. Copans, *Critiques et politiques de l'anthropologie*, Paris 1974.

famous phrase from the original French version of the *Internationale* reflects the linear view of human progress that characterized the naïve rationalism of the nineteenth century! A society will always need to define its past — will always need its past to define its future. . . .

Index